Aelred of Rievaulx

... je cherche l'amour. L'amour comme un vertige,
comme un sacrifice et comme le dernier mot sur
tout. La chose après quoi rien n'existe. Le depart,
après avoir mis le feu aux quatre coins du pays.

ALAIN-FOURNIER

MS Douai 392, fol. 3r, the opening words of the text of Aelred's *Mirror of Charity*, formerly belonging to the abbey of Anchin. This is probably the only surviving medieval representation of Aelred. He is depicted in relation to St Bernard, whose figure, seated in the act of writing, faces him from the opposite page.

AELRED
OF RIEVAULX
A STUDY

Aelred Squire, O.P.

LONDON

S·P·C·K

1969

First published in 1969
by S.P.C.K.
Holy Trinity Church
Marylebone Road
London N.W.1

Made and printed in Great Britain by
William Clowes and Sons, Limited
London and Beccles

SBN 281 02339 5

To my Mother

CONTENTS

PREFACE

This study of an unusually engaging English twelfth-century abbot has been taking shape for over twenty years. It is what it says it is: a study—one of several possible ways of looking at what we know about its subject. While it is the fruit of attending closely to the historical sources, even in matters about which it chooses to be silent, it does not aim at history or biography in the more usual sense. The qualities of writing of that kind are already admirably combined in the late Sir Maurice Powicke's edition of Walter Daniel's *Life of Ailred*. This study tries rather to establish a mood of listening to the resonances of a life bound by its own particular conventions, as all lives are, yet discovering its personal liberation and authenticity in a manner which may often seem surprisingly instructive to very different people in nevertheless kindred situations. Some may prefer to take their history for granted and enjoy an exercise in communication and sympathy. Intrusive commentary and criticism is consciously avoided and Aelred is allowed to speak for himself as much as possible. Those who, on the other hand, may wish to weigh the evidence further for themselves will find the fundamental sources sparingly but, it is hoped, sufficiently indicated in the notes at the end. The index is meant to perform a real function in tracing the echoes of the themes in which the book abounds.

It was Dom Albert Derzelle, monk of Chimay and, at the time when I first knew him, prior of the abbey of Caldey off the Pembrokeshire coast, who gave the first discreet yet decided encouragement to my interest in early Cistercian studies, and particularly in Aelred. To his kindness and insight, then and later, I owe more than he suspects. During the same long period I have enjoyed the friendship of Père Charles Dumont and profited, I trust, from our many long discussions about Aelred's life and teaching. In his quiet old chaplaincy at Chimay the first pages of this book were written.

My debt to three Oxford scholars is of a different but equally important kind. Professor R. W. Southern supervised my research degree on Aelred with endless patience and generosity. Miss Beryl Smalley brought me to the point of really planning a book. Those who come and go in the Bodleian Library over the years will not be surprised at the consistent help I have received from Dr Richard Hunt. It is hard to imagine how so busy a man manages to remember what everyone is studying and what little details of information will be of value and interest to each. While none of these scholars is in any way responsible for this book's defects, any solid virtues it may have are largely due to their advice and example.

A member of a Religious Order has debts to his own brethren too numerous to specify, but I ought particularly to mention the Brothers at Blackfriars, Oxford, in my time there, who protected me from the importunities of the telephone and the doorbell, and Fr Fergus Kerr, who looked after the affairs of the completed text when I was working abroad.

The Reverend A. M. Allchin, Librarian of Pusey House, was always my neighbour in a more than physical sense, and it was his conviction of the interest of this study that ultimately found it a publisher. The Reverend Michael Perry of the S.P.C.K. has shown me nothing but kindness about everything connected with the book's production, my brother Geoffrey has drawn the map, and Dom Alberic Stacpoole of Ampleforth Abbey has taken infinite pains about many points that needed re-thinking and revision. Without the help of these and of many friends of whom I do not speak, this book could never have come into existence.

St Catherine's Centre,   Aelred Squire, O.P.
Portobello Road, W.10

1
Vocation

On the night of 12 January 1167 the body of Aelred, abbot of Rievaulx, who had just died, was stripped to be washed and prepared
for burial. He had been a very sick man for ten years and more and
crippled with arthritis, yet the monk who, the previous day, had
held the dying man's head in his hands during some of his last
moments of consciousness, thought he had never seen a lovelier
sight than the body of his abbot in its final repose. It was typical of
him that his account of Aelred's life should say this in words almost
entirely borrowed from a book that such a man would naturally
have had in mind.[1] For no work had had a more continuous influence on the way the lives of saints were told in the Latin Christian
West than the early fifth-century life of St Martin by Sulpicius
Severus. It had become one of the documents in the case for seeing
the monks and ascetics of later days as the true inheritors of that
ardent Christian faith which had led the early martyrs to their
sufferings. Walter Daniel is less of an instinctive artist with words
than his dead master and friend and, in his desire to depict Aelred's
life according to the accepted canons of hagiography and sound
learning, is unwilling to waste anything he knows that might give
weight to his argument. He will, for instance, make a description of
Aelred's prayer the occasion for airing his own acquaintance with
topics that interested contemporary philosophers, remote though
they may be from any distraction that could conceivably have
occurred to Aelred himself.[2] Yet it was his undisguised claim that
Aelred, in life and in death, was worthy to be numbered in the
company of men like Martin of Tours that loosened the tongues
of the critics remarkable men never fail to find about them. A letter

of rejoinder, which admits his literary debt to Sulpicius Severus, may be taken as the measure of the combative, possessive sincerity which animates and often breaks through even Walter Daniel's borrowed phrases, as when he tells us of the compulsive kisses with which he covered the dead man's feet. A more overt demonstration, he says, might credibly have been attributed to a sentimental impulse rather than to genuine love. The suggestion of awed restraint leaves us in no doubt that Walter really believed himself to have seen that transfiguration of the body by the spirit which is often the accompaniment of real goodness. Of the ultimate outcome he need not have been afraid. Although he was never formally canonized, Aelred was to be continuously venerated by his brethren and the people of England as a saint, and in the sixteenth century, before the dissolution of the monastery, John Leland saw at Rievaulx the shrine containing Aelred's body glittering with gold and silver.[3]

Aelred's posthumous fame was not, in any case, dependent upon the fluctuating chances of his human reputation. For he had left behind him writings on various topics sufficient to establish his perennial interest both for historians and Christians with problems and attractions like his own, and this has been increasingly recognized. Yet the anxious care of Walter Daniel to preserve the portrait of a man he had loved was by no means superfluous. His plausible reminders of very different reactions to Aelred's character bring us close to a life that, in the concrete, had evidently not been all vision and romance. Walter's *Life* gives us a framework and a rough chronology into which to fit the output of Aelred's career as a writer. He preserves in addition, embedded in his anecdotes, a number of sayings of Aelred whose authenticity may be judged against Aelred's own words in other places. None is circumstantially more revealing than a little phrase that escapes the abbot in a prediction about the day of his death. "On the day before the ides of January my soul, *the handmaid of the Lord*, will migrate from this its earthly home where it has so far dwelt.[4] In these words Aelred suggests the dispositions of his own soul at the moment of death by allusion to the words of the Virgin Mary in the moment of her Annunciation. They are so unexpectedly telling in a narrative where the great images of scripture never intervene with any notable force, that they can scarcely be contrived. They must certainly represent something Aelred had genuinely said of himself.

"Alas for us!", we find him saying to his monks in one of his sermons for the feast of the Annunciation,

Of whose soul, pray, is this the expression? *Behold the handmaid of the Lord.* Which of us does not rather seek that wretched liberty of which the apostle says, *when you were the servants of sin, then were you free with regard to justice?* And can that soul which loves its own will, which never says to its Father Prior, *Be it done unto me according to thy word,* be a handmaid, until either in the heart or in these very words that expression suggests the idea?[5]

This is the authentic Aelred, from whose imagination, long disciplined by hours of meditation and reflection, the symbols and images of scripture rise as the most adequate expression of the operative realities in his own life and experience. If his response to the personal annunciation of God's calling had led him to embrace in a monastery a form of Christian life of which the virtue of obedience is the conscious centre, there are reasons for supposing that he had come to see the claim of his vocation upon him as more extensive and far-reaching still. In a prayer he had written as abbot he speaks of his desire that nothing in his soul should be hidden from the eyes of God, the searcher of hearts, and begs that everything about him should in some way be used for the good of those to whom his pastoral duty commits him.

What I feel, what I say, my leisure and my employment, what I do and what I think, my good fortune and my ill, my death and my life, my health and my sickness, whatever I am in any way, the fact that I live, feel, perceive, let it all be available for them and all be spent for them for whom thou thyself didst not disdain to be spent.[6]

This is clearly the way in which Aelred in his mature years envisaged the meaning of his entire formation and of all that had happened to him however insignificant, so that, in doing what he believed to be God's will, he had eventually found his personal fulfilment. We need not suppose that he had always been so conscious as he ultimately became of the part that so many different factors, cultural, psychological, and spiritual, had played in making him what he was, but his instincts had always led him towards their complete integration, as the works he left behind him bear witness. There is really nothing about his life that is not given value and does not find a place among them. In a time of change, when self-awareness was an asset, Aelred was by family and birth intimately connected with the still vital traditions of the past, while in politics and religion he was identified with all that was new. In his personal development old and new conduct an amicable dialogue.

Aelred was born at Hexham in 1110,[7] in a place and of a family acutely conscious of its links with a very remote past. Northumbria, where Hexham lay, was originally the name applied rather vaguely to all the land north of the Humber. It had had a long history as an independent kingdom that at some periods stretched from the Yorkshire wolds as far north as the Firth of Forth and Bede, who probably never went beyond its borders, is its great historian. Behind him in the line of Northumbrian historians lie the biographers of the two greatest figures of the Northern Kingdom in the seventh century, Wilfrid and Cuthbert. There was a sharp contrast between the personalities of these two men—Wilfrid, the champion of Roman ways, whose episcopal state could be described as resembling that of a king, and Cuthbert, the former shepherd-boy, whose Celtic simplicity had earned him an authority of a more endearing kind— but in the popular imagination these differences tended to be lost in their common reputation for sanctity, and to a pious Hexham boy in the early years of the twelfth century they could still appear to be the real powers in the land. Of the many stories of their continued interventions which Aelred either told to his friends or committed to writing in middle age, one that belongs only to the days of his grandfather depicts the two saints riding together to the rescue of the defenceless little town that had suffered generations of violence from armed men appearing out of the mist across the Tyne.[8] Not that even to a Hexham man Wilfrid and Cuthbert could normally have seemed to be quite equals in power in Aelred's day, when the hold of St Cuthbert over the lands about Durham was something the Normans themselves were compelled to take seriously. Nevertheless, at Wilfrid's old sanctuary of Hexham the Danish invasions of the ninth century, which appear to have ensured the extinction of the ancient bishopric there, had not obliterated the memory of its associations with him or destroyed all traces of those architectural achievements which had been the pride and joy of his heart. On Queen Aethelthryth's grant of royal dower land, sometime between 672–78, he had set out to build a little Rome in the north.[9] The crypt beneath his church of St Andrew still survives, and when Aelred was a boy there was more to see, for Wilfrid's church above it was still standing, and someone—presumably a relative of Aelred—had restored the shattered church of our Lady which, built in the form of a Greek cross with drum-like central tower, had occupied Wilfrid's closing years. William of Malmesbury, writing in Aelred's youth, reports how travellers who knew Rome itself, were still being astonished at these monumental signs of Wilfrid's devotion to Hexham.[10] As for Aelred, he continued to imagine that these buildings were only splendid replacements of others that went back to the days of forgotten kings.[11]

With Cuthbert, however, he must have felt a more intimate tie. In 875 the bishop of Lindisfarne, where the incorrupt body of Cuthbert lay, had decided that flight before the threat of the Danes was the course of action the saint himself had prophesied the community would one day be compelled to take.[12] Therefore, taking the precious body and a few other treasures, including the *Lindisfarne Gospels*, a little party of clerics and their families set out on a kind of desert pilgrimage from one place of refuge to another. The coffin of St Cuthbert travelled with them, rather like the Ark of the Covenant, and special bearers were appointed to carry it. From them, a twelfth-century Durham historian tells us, many clerics and laymen in his day were proud to descend.[13] It looks as though Aelred must have come of one of these families. As an older man he told Reginald of Durham some stories of the hardships of these wandering years, when the shrine-bearers were once reduced to nothing but a horse's head and a large cheese for food,[14] and he certainly appears to have claimed the kind of special knowledge of the fortunes of the saint's body in the late ninth and tenth centuries that its custodians might be expected to have. After being settled at Chester-le-Street for more than a century from 883, Cuthbert's body had finally been removed with the bishops of the see to Durham in 995,[15] and there, in a man acting as sacrist and shrine-keeper, we make our first certain contact with an ancestor of Aelred. For a good many years in the first half of the eleventh century Alfred son of Westou, Aelred's great-grandfather, clearly held an important place in the succession of faithful guardians of St Cuthbert's body.[16] Stories about him were circulating in Durham more than fifty years later. He had held the key to Cuthbert's coffin and combed and trimmed the saint's hair and beard and cut his fingernails. It was a well-known fact among his friends that he would thus acquire hairs which would pass the test of being placed on the coals prepared for the incense, where they would glow like burnished gold, without shrivelling in the heat. He was, indeed, a somewhat unscrupulous connoisseur of the authentic relic, and confided to his intimates that, if anyone were searching for the bones of Bede, it might be good advice to look in St Cuthbert's coffin. It had cost him a few days' solitary vigil among the ruins of Jarrow, and a hasty departure at dawn, to obtain them without anyone's knowledge. Other places in Northumbria were also the object of these pious predatory excursions, but traditions differed as to how far portions of the relics the Durham sacrist unearthed found their way to the safe keeping of the coffin of St Cuthbert. It was presumably in connection with a prolonged absence on quests of this kind that Aelred's own father told him how Alfred had received a rather testy complaint from the saint that a weasel was rearing a family in his coffin. Her gentle reaction to discovery saved her life and vindicated the power of the saint in the eyes of the flustered custodian and his family after him. To them the presence of the saints, whether to assist or punish, was something quasi-physical, as it needed to be in lives that were constantly harassed by harsh physical fact. Aelred was brought up to believe that his great-grandfather's immoderate interest in relics was nothing less than a response to a divine vocation singularly comprehensible in its day. Not that Alfred son of Westou was lacking in refinements and learning of a kind. He had been known as *larwa*, the Northumbrian form of a Saxon word that means *teacher*, for at Durham he instructed the boys in the elements of music and letters necessary for performing the liturgy. But his was evidently a robust, old-fashioned piety that throve on the frequent recitation of the psalter and had about it a touch of something that could put the fear of God even into a bishop. Bishop Edmund of Durham (1023–36) had given him the living of Hexham for which, since his duties kept him elsewhere, he instituted curates.[17] He lived on into the time of bishop Aethelwine, leaving Hexham to his son Eilaf, who continued his father's arrangements there, until developments which led to his taking up residence himself.

Aethelwine's episcopate coincided with the Norman Conquest, which was nowhere more stubbornly resisted than in Northumbria. Physical inaccessibility and a resilient sense of local tradition naturally made it a difficult area to handle, and in the sudden, hard winter of 1068 the spirit of resistance around Durham was stiffened by news of an approaching Norman force. Bishop Aethelwine, who seems at first to have been pro-Norman in sympathy, warned the king's men of their danger, but they came on. On 28 January 1069, after a single night in Durham, they were surprised at dawn and cut to pieces, their leader being burnt alive in the bishop's house, where he had spent the night. Heartened by the news, the local forces immediately made an attack on York. This was a situation which required the Conqueror's personal intervention and the Durham historian describes the horror that followed in its wake, the bodies of the dead rotting by the wayside, the whole country between York and Durham deserted, save for the refugees who were ready to eat anything they could lay hands on, dogs, cats, horses, and even human flesh. Bishop Aethelwine, fearing the appearance of implication in the English resistance, fled to Lindisfarne with his clerics and took the body of St Cuthbert with him, so that in Durham the cathedral became simply a shelter for the sick and dying.[18] Since Aelred's grandfather, Eilaf, was a Durham *larwa*, like his father before him, there seems no reason to suppose that he did not go with the rest of the clergy. Significantly Aelred later had once again a personal contribution to make to the story of this last of the many journeys of the body of St Cuthbert.[19] It was a brief interlude and the clergy were back at Durham by the beginning of Lent 1070. But it was long enough for their bishop to make up his mind that the new régime, with its foreign language and foreign ways, was not for him.[20] He was to maintain his position—the only English bishop known to have done so—until his death in monastic confinement at Abingdon, and shortly his clergy would be faced with a similar choice.

The Norman nominee appointed to Durham in 1071 was bishop Walcher, a Lotharingian. In his own duchy William the Conqueror had long been identified, in a manner that was no disadvantage to him, with that movement for Church reform which was shortly to capture the papal throne in the person of Gregory VII. Any bishop William chose could be expected to share the views that were in the ascendency. At Durham bishop Walcher found a situation that must have surprised him: a cathedral administered by clergy accustomed to reciting their Office like the monks their ancestors had once been, but now respectably married with families of their own. It must have been a warning to Aelred's grandfather that there was more to come when the bishop began by reforming the cathedral Offices to those of the secular canons.[21] To insist on a celibate staff at this point would clearly have been impossible, but a providential occurrence was soon going to suggest a solution. At the monastery of Winchcombe in the Cotswolds the imagination of the prior, Aldwin, had been fired by what he had read of the ancient monastic life of Northumbria and its saints, and in 1073 he, and two like-minded monks from Evesham, set out in absolute poverty with the object of reviving this religious life in the north. Hearing of their arrival, and recognizing the quality of the men he was dealing with, Walcher was prompt to offer them his protection. He settled them at the ruined monastery of Jarrow, content to await the development of future possibilities.[22] He himself was not to see them realized. Following on the complicity of the Northumbrian earl in an anti-Norman plot hatched in 1075, the king tried the experiment of solving his northern problems by vesting the bishop with the civil and military rights and duties of the earldom. It was a step which ultimately led to Walcher's murder by an enraged mob at Gateshead in 1080. Thither bishop Odo of Bayeux was sent to administer the king's revenge, which he did with a severity that left Northumbria desolate once again. Within six months a young and vigorous successor to Walcher, William of St Carilef, had been appointed at Durham. He would settle the affairs of the old Durham clergy with a firm hand. Bishop Walcher had begun to erect monastic buildings next to the cathedral and William of St Carilef decided it was time for them to be occupied. In 1083, by the authority of Gregory VII himself, the monks from Jarrow were brought to Durham and the older clergy were given the option of becoming monks or leaving.[23] All but one refused to stay, among them Aelred's grandfather, Eilaf.

He was doubtless prepared for this eventuality, and the disturbed times since Aethelwine's episcopate had favoured his plans. The provost of Hexham during that period had already suggested to Thomas, the first Norman archbishop of York, that a renewal of the old connection between the two places was both desirable and possible. No one at Durham seemed interested, and now in 1083 it was to York that Eilaf turned for help. Under an alternative religious superior he might at least be able to keep his Hexham living. And so it was that the family moved out there. At Hexham, as elsewhere in Northumbria, Odo of Bayeux' revenge for the murder of bishop Walcher had left its mark. Aelred must often

have heard what the place looked like when his grandfather first
arrived there.

> Coming to the place [Aelred wrote later] he found everything
> deserted, the walls of the roofless church clogged with grass, and the
> woods encroaching all over it. A sorry sight on account of the dirt, the
> rains and the storms, it had no trace of its former beauty left. Such
> indeed was the desolation of those parts that for almost two years he
> was able to keep himself and his family by hunting and fowling
> alone.[24]

Meanwhile at Durham, in a setting less retired than any of the
three founders had originally aspired to, the new community
prospered. By this time, indeed, the initiative of 1073 had led to
monastic foundations at Wearmouth and at Whitby. Thence, about
1078, a group had founded St Mary's, York, a house whose later
fortunes would have a special interest for Aelred, when some of its
members followed an inspiration similar to that which lay behind
the Northumbrian monastic revival of his grandfather's day. New
ideas and new men needed to express themselves in new buildings
and, from 1093 onwards, a new cathedral which was to be a con-
summate expression of Norman *savoir-faire*, began to rise on the
rock at Durham. Aelred seems to have told Reginald of Durham of
a family tradition that his great-grandfather had long ago predicted
the erection of this magnificent building,[25] the east end of which was
sufficiently complete in 1104 to make possible a solemn translation
of the body of St Cuthbert to its new shrine.[26] Gone was what
Reginald of Durham euphemistically called the "innocent simplicity" of former days, but it must have been some satisfaction to
the family in charge of the church at Hexham that, whatever the
shortcomings of the modern world, Cuthbert had at least been given
his rightful place in it.

At Hexham, resources for honouring the bones of the English
saints were less abundant. Eilaf *Lawra* had been full of good intentions, but evidently the struggle for existence meant that at the time
of his death he had done little more than erect a decent altar at the
east end of the ruined church, where he could fulfil his priestly
functions. His son, Aelred's father, another Eilaf, got to work with
greater energy, repairing the roof with tiles, cleaning the walls in-
side and out, and laying a new sanctuary floor beneath a more
seemly altar supported on columns. For a time he put his young

brother Aldred in charge of the relics of the Hexham saints, whose bones he eventually enclosed in a casket as fitting as he could provide. But there he reached his limit. Even in Durham itself there seems to have been a pause in the building operations about the year 1110, the year in which Aelred was born. Whether from lack of funds or of determined direction, now that William of St Carilef was dead, the nave of the cathedral was not to be finished until 1133, when Aelred was a young man in his twenties.[27] But by the time he was three there had been yet another change at Hexham which led to the erection of new buildings there.

It appears that, already in the time of the first Norman archbishop Thomas, Hexham had been granted to a prebend of York, so that Aelred's father continued his ministrations simply as a curate living on part of the income. To a second archbishop Thomas, appointed in 1108, the situation at Hexham seemed to call for further changes and he resolved to take a step which would come naturally to a reform-minded archbishop in those days. In 1113 he gave Hexham to the nucleus of a house of canons, leaving Eilaf with the parochial cure and a sufficient revenue for his needs. Both Aelred and the canons of Hexham later make a conscious endeavour to put the kindliest interpretation on the facts as they see them. Aelred declares that his father, concerned at the inadequacy with which he fulfilled his responsibilities to his ancient church, actually asked the archbishop to send the canons; they, in their turn, profess to be mollified for the years of hardship they had endured on a depleted income by a touching scene that took place in Durham in 1138. In that year Eilaf, perhaps on a visit to Durham friends and relatives, collapsed in what was obviously his last illness. Summoning the Hexham prior of the day, and using a silver reliquary cross containing bones of Hexham saints as a sign of the transaction, Eilaf surrendered to him the family interest, while the three sons, Samuel, Ethelwold, and Aelred stood by among the witnesses. Of the other brothers we know nothing, but Aelred himself had by this time already been a monk for some four years and was present for the occasion with his abbot. His father lingered for a time, making a death-bed profession as a monk of St Cuthbert's community. How far these scenes of final reconciliation to the representatives of the new forces in the land are to be taken as the happy term of about fifty years of underground resistance to the inevitable on the part of Eilaf and his father before him, it is hard to judge. But certainly

Aelred and Richard of Hexham, upon whom we depend for our
facts, both make it clear through their very efforts to be fair to Eilaf
that there are other matters upon which they preserve a studied
reticence. When Aelred refers to his father as "a sinner", we should
probably be correct in assuming that this expresses his disapproval
of a married clergy, though, naturally, to Eilaf himself the demand
for celibacy would seem to be a new one. Most of his life he would
have felt no guilt on that score, any more than other priests whose
marriages continued to be accepted by their neighbours as entirely
regular and respectable. Presumably it was someone in Durham
who gave him another conscience on that subject as he lay dying, if
this is to be taken as the meaning of his contrition for years of
misappropriation of the Hexham revenues. Nevertheless it remains
obscure whether it was something more than his shifts to support a
family that drew on him the fire of criticism. Richard of Hexham
reports with obvious satisfaction the fact that the canons had been
tolerant of the situation at Hexham for more than twenty years,
though they could easily have taken a tougher line with the curate
if they had wished to do so. If there were tensions and unedifying
episodes during his earliest years, it is probable that many of these
would be lost on Aelred as a small boy. He would scarcely
appreciate a double meaning in his father's retort at the announce-
ment of the death of archbishop Thomas II that "he is dead who
lives an evil life",[28] if this was intended by Eilaf as an oblique
reference to another version of the arrival of the Hexham canons
than that charitably believed by his son. Eilaf had, it seems, a touch
of the spirit of the days that were passing that one could not fail to
like and admire, and even to the canons he seemed paternal.

To Aelred he was the source of that sense of a personal link with
a distant past which was fostered by the stories Eilaf told about his
family. It was these which captured the boy's imagination, as much
as the atmosphere of the tales and marks of antiquity about the old
buildings at Hexham, and he cherished a host of picturesque details
about his ancestry which make it possible, again and again, to give
life to their story over more than one troubled century. That he
spoke of them as freely as he evidently did, suggests that next to a
profound gratitude for being born of Christian parents which he
later spoke of to his sister,[29] he felt a pride in all that was positive
about the sturdy English stock from which he had come. If he is
silent about any of his father's differences with the canons, he

remembers to tell us that it was Eilaf who prepared the first wooden buildings for them with his own hands.[30] He would doubtless seem a bit of a rustic beside the canon Asketill from Huntingdon in the south, whom the new archbishop Thurstan appointed as prior soon after his accession to York in 1114, and of whose civilizing and conciliatory qualities Aelred has warm words of praise which are certainly based on personal memories. Nevertheless, Eilaf was not the son of an old Durham teacher for nothing and it may well have been he, or his younger brother Aldred, reputed in Durham to be well-versed in holy scripture,[31] who taught Aelred his first letters. For that Eilaf was a practical protagonist of the culture of the old Saxon and Celtic tradition emerges from the fact that it was the life of St Bridget he gave to Aelred's friend Laurence, the writer and monk of Durham, which lies behind one of the new Durham books later dedicated to Aelred. That Aelred himself reached the position of detached enthusiasm about his family which reveals itself in what he wrote and said about them was due to a more decisive factor in his upbringing than anything about his earliest years at Hexham.

It is unfortunate that we only know in the most general terms of the beginnings of Aelred's association with the family and entourage of King David of Scotland. How the first contact was made, whether directly through Eilaf, through one of Aelred's Durham relatives, or through one of the Hexham canons is not clear. But, at a time when relations between Northumbria and Scotland were close, and when representatives of Scottish royalty were often to be found in Durham, it cannot have been difficult. Whatever persuaded the king to do so, he adopted Aelred into the royal household and had him brought up with his son Henry, and his two stepsons, Simon and Waldef. Aelred was just fourteen when David became king in 1124, and it may be to a date about then that Aelred refers when in his lament for David he says that he had known him "from the beginning of his age". It is true that he also speaks of his friendship for prince Henry as though they had been cradle companions, but this probably means no more than that Henry was nearest to Aelred in age. Jocelyn of Furness, in his life of Waldef, implies that in order to join the king's court Aelred left whatever school he was attending before the normal time.[32] But, if Aelred's own account of how he lost his heart first to one boy and then to another during his school days refers to his initial schooling,[33] it would scarcely be plausible to suppose that he was much less than twelve at the time, and again fourteen is a more probable age. We must not forget, however, that he was going to no ordinary court and, even if the formal discipline of the schoolroom came to an end early for him, we need not suppose that his general formation among his noble friends was by any means neglected. At the old Scottish capital, Roxburgh, tutors would surely be available, perhaps from among the Tironese monks, whom David had brought to Selkirk while he was still an earl and who, removed to Kelso, would soon own a Roxburgh school.[34] However it may be, among the pursuits whereby Aelred was expected to acquire "the royal virtues which he afterwards described for the solace of the faithful"[35] reading was certainly included. There is a story, sufficiently in character not to be a hagiographical invention, of how Waldef, whose friendship was probably vital to Aelred at a decisive moment in his life, would find a way of evading his part in the royal hunt and, passing on the king's bow to someone else, would slip away into a tree with a book.[36] On Aelred, whose emotional life was just awakening, personal example was never lost. Later in life he speaks like a man who has, in youth, seen in the people he has known and admired that it is possible to realize the ideal. As boys will, Aelred's companions gave imaginative expression to their enthusiasms in their play, Simon building castles of branches, while Waldef built churches and simulated the sounds and gestures of the officiating clergy. It was after he became a monk that Aelred found an occasion for paying tribute to the perfect, chivalrous knight that Henry had become. But he was appreciative of the virtues of them all and, under the discerning patronage of king David, his life expanded in an atmosphere of friendship. The adaptation to Norman ways which had been so long and difficult a process for his father, and so late and so imperfectly accomplished, was made easy for him at the court of this king. Born a Scot, David had been brought up in England in the household of Henry I and of his own sister, Henry's sophisticated, francophile Queen Matilda, where he had "rubbed off all the rust of his Scots barbarity".[37] To David the Norman way was the normal way to do things and it was natural that he should see to it that his stepson Waldef spoke French as well as he spoke English.[38] This was the medium through which so much that was new flowed across the Channel. This, then, became the normal world for Aelred too, the world he could more easily take for granted than the one into which he had been born, since he was absorbing its new values at a time when the mind is most impressionable and in the company of men the memory of whom always remained the dearest thing in his life. His biographer, Walter Daniel, makes the most of the function at court to which the king's favour promoted Aelred when he was old enough to be given it, and hints at talk that the young man would have risen to a bishopric in due course, had he bided his time. But if his office were really so distinguished, it is surprising that his name does not appear once as a witness on any of the surviving acts of king David,[39] and a more natural interpretation of the facts is that Aelred was steward in the king's banqueting-hall, supervising the running of the meals,[40] a function in which there was a place for the exercise of that tact and gentleness in promoting the ease and well-being of others, which had been remarked in him from his youth. It was evidently his wont to say in later life that he knew more about catering than anything else, and he offered it among his excuses for not settling down to write his first book. Later too, when he was an abbot, the young Durham friend, Reginald, to whom he had told many stories of St Cuthbert, found a neat way of dedicating his book to Aelred by relating the abbot's former function at court to his present pastoral duty to provide his monks with food of another kind. "To his devoted father and lord, Aelred, royal dispenser in the house of the Lord,"[41] he wrote. There was, in any case, a considerable amount of exaggeration in Aelred's plea that he spent all his time in the kitchen for, even during the period while he was still *dispenser* at David's court, a book was dedicated to him in which the author, Laurence, a Durham monk who had known his father Eilaf, declares he is aware that Aelred is "accustomed to have a care for letters." The truth of this is verified by Aelred's own admission that it was in his youth that he came to know and admire Cicero's dialogue *On Friendship*, not the kind of book that a genuinely illiterate man would be able even to read, much less to enjoy. But it is evident that neither then, nor later in life, was Aelred ever indifferent to ideas and the way they were expressed, especially if they made a contribution to his reflections on a subject which remained a passionate interest all his life long.

For it seems that his youth brought with it a painful initiation into the problems of love. He was, to begin with, a man of very strong emotional sensibility. This will be clear enough from many passages in his writings, and we know from an evidently auto-

biographical passage in a work addressed to his sister that the
strength of his physical passions persuaded him of the need to
adopt, at one period, the old Celtic ascetic practice of immersion in
cold water.[42] But it would seem that it was not the crude force of his
feelings which caused him the greatest difficulty. We shall find his
first work, the *Mirror of Charity*, faithful in its reflection of the
excitement he felt at the discovery of the possibilities of human
relationship. There, too, we find his only attempt to describe the
state of emotional conflict to which, in his days at king David's
court, these relationships could reduce him. The boy who had easily
lost his heart to his fellows went on doing so. But now, when he
gave himself with his adult passion, he became aware of desires
which human love could awaken and sustain, but never satisfy. He
describes himself as held, during these years, by a friendship which
was at once "dearer to me than all the delights of this life", and yet
a source of torment. "For some offence was always to be feared,
and a parting, sometime in the future, was a certainty." While to
others he seemed to swim in universal favour, he found himself
caught between ideals he was compelled to strive for and longings
he could neither gratify nor transform. Looking back on it all afterwards, it seemed to him that if God, through the turn of events,
had not provided him with the opportunity of working out a solution, his state of mind would have been suicidal.[43]

Aelred was little more than eighteen when he had his first taste
of a parting in the intimate circle in which he had matured. Waldef
took a decision of a kind which must long have been foreseen by
joining the community of canons in the Yorkshire woods at
Nostell.[44] For Aelred the way was still not clear. He could doubtless
sympathize with Waldef's sense of vocation, but the ties with the
familiar life of the court, and with the friend he loved so extrava-
gantly, were not yet to be loosened. He who appreciated so vividly
what a man looked like and how his whole bearing revealed his
mind still needed to experience the immediate impact of a group of
men who could compete for his allegiance with those he already
knew. This experience came to him, not perhaps without some
discreet manoeuvring behind the scenes, in the course of carrying
out a commission for king David which took Aelred to see a man
who had European contacts with much that was new and alive in
the Church, archbishop Thurstan of York.

From his youth Thurstan had been attracted by the religious life,

and the one personal event we know of before his appointment to
York in 1114 is of a visit to Cluny, still the monastic centre of
Europe in the days of the great St Hugh, a visit during which he
promised eventually to take the Cluniac habit. It was a promise
which, in spite of the blandishments of St Bernard, he kept when
he died in the habit at Pontefract in 1140. Apart from his refusal to
acknowledge any dependence of his see on that of Canterbury—a
stand which soon took him off on many journeys abroad—one of
his first concerns on his appointment as archbishop had been to
further the progress of the reformed canonical life in the places
under his control. Thus at Hexham he had promptly found a suitable man from Huntingdon, one of the eleventh-century pioneer
houses of reformed clerical life, a canon who could not only push
ahead with stone buildings for the community, but form his subjects in the best traditions of the religious life. Thurstan later
showed them his favour by gifts of relics, books, church ornaments,
and grants of land, and saw to it that one of the canons became a
prebend of his cathedral church at York.[45] He had also interested
himself as early as 1114 in another group of canons who had settled
south of York at Nostell in a place formerly used by hermits.[46] By
1119 their buildings were going up and a letter of royal favour
makes it clear that they were officially living under the rule of
St Augustine. The evolution of this house is characteristic of a trend
towards the canonical life which was the spontaneous expression of
a widely felt need for a reformed clergy. On this, half a century
earlier, archdeacon Hildebrand had been eloquent, years before he
became pope Gregory VII. It was only gradually that the so-called
rule of St Augustine, really hardly more than a letter of advice,
came to be generally accepted as the basis of the canonical life.[47]
Initially at Nostell, as also at a more famous house like that of
St Victor in Paris, founded in 1108, the inspiration had clearly been
to provide a more austere contemplative life for clerks living in
common. Such houses were shortly to be over-shadowed by others
springing from a more radically monastic root, and going much
further in their quest for solitude and contemplation. David of
Scotland had discovered one group of this kind while he was still
Earl of Huntingdon, when he had brought the monks of Tiron to
Selkirk in 1113. These monks were only one manifestation of a
notable movement towards reformed monastic life which had led a
number of men of different origins out into the woods of Maine

and Brittany in the closing years of the eleventh century. It is probable that some of them knew that further south in Burgundy a similar inspiration had already been at work.

There again, everything had begun with a group of hermits living in the woods not far from Langres. They had invited an abbot, Robert, to govern them and about 1075 the community began life at Molesme in huts made from the trees. By 1098 twenty of them felt so strongly that the original simplicity of their purposes had gone that, with Robert at their head, they started again in the woods of Cîteaux. After a crisis in which Robert eventually had to agree to return to the parent community, they survived under an Englishman, Stephen Harding, who was their abbot from 1109. They were heartened in 1112 by the arrival of the young St Bernard with thirty companions. Archbishop Thurstan of York was in the train of pope Calixtus II when in 1119 he approved the way of life of the monks of Cîteaux in a document which has recently become a matter for discussion.[48] What these monks stood for from the beginning is, however, clear. In their new grey-white habit they desired to return to what they saw as the primitive sources of their monastic life, above all the Rule of St Benedict observed without mitigations and without the heavy liturgical accretions which had become characteristic of the life of the monks of Cluny. They intended to do regular manual labour, to avoid all feudal and ecclesiastical entanglements and, although this was strictly speaking contrary to St Benedict's rule, to have nothing to do with the education of boys and youths who might disturb the peace of the cloister. Thurstan can scarcely have guessed in 1119 what a great future the white monks of Cîteaux had before them, and what a disturbance they would cause when they arrived in his diocese.

Meanwhile, between 1128–30, Aelred's companion Waldef had joined the canons at Nostell. Could he have set eyes on the little group of Cistercians who, under the patronage of the bishop of Winchester, began their life at Waverley in Surrey at the end of 1128, he might already have felt the impulse that was later to lead him to join their observance. But, as Aelred once found occasion to say, Waverley was "lost in a corner",[49] nor had it behind it the drive which arranged for the arrival of the Cistercians in Yorkshire sometime in 1131. Archbishop Thurstan cannot have failed to know of, even if he was not actually involved in, the negotiations which had been going on between Bernard of Clairvaux, Henry I, and Walter

Espec, the founder of Rievaulx, since the official foundation was
made on 5 March 1132 "with Thurstan's advice and approval."[50]
Bernard had chosen his shock-troops carefully, placing at their head
an Englishman, William, who had been his secretary, and sending
with him a number of Yorkshiremen who had found their way to
Clairvaux. They were to live in a valley site of the type Cistercians
generally chose, on the river Rye, not far from their founder's castle
at Helmsley, "a second paradise of wooded delight", as Walter
Daniel calls it.[51]

It was only a matter of months before the presence of these men
in their huts among the trees twenty-five miles away had divided
the community of St Mary's, York, down the middle. To some the
new way of life seemed a real challenge of conscience, and when it
was discovered that these included the prior and the sub-prior, it
was decided to lay the matter before the abbot. All they asked, prior
Richard declared, was to be allowed to follow "the ancient rule of
our blessed father Benedict, nay rather the most ancient gospel of
Christ, which precedes all rules",[52] and discontinue those customs
which seemed to them to contravene it, "the delicious joints, the
different flavoured spices, the variety of dishes" and other comforts.
Behind them the would-be reformers had the support of archbishop
Thurstan, upon a letter from whom we depend for our more de-
tailed knowledge of what the contending parties said. There was
doubtless more to be said for the conservative point of view than
has generally been recognized either then or since,[53] for no genuinely
relaxed abbey produces so many men to whom ideas like these
would make much appeal. But Thurstan, who was discreet enough
to go to the Black monks in the end, could not resist the attraction
of the standards the white monks set, and was prepared to pay the
price for his enthusiasm. When, after facing a packed and stormy
chapter meeting at St Mary's on 17 October 1133, it proved impossible to negotiate any compromise, Thurstan took those who
desired a more austere way of life under his protection. He gave
them the land on which the abbey of Fountains was finally built.
There he supported them through the long period while negotiations were conducted for their entry into the Cistercian order, and
they awaited an influx of recruits, some of whom, from among his
own clergy of York itself, would prove wealthy enough to ensure
the survival of the community.

Archbishop Thurstan, then, the man to whom Aelred was sent about 1134 on an unspecified errand for King David of Scotland,[54] was no passive spectator of events which everyone was discussing. The probability is that Aelred's mission concerned an interminable dispute between Thurstan and David's old tutor John, Bishop of Glasgow, who refused to acknowledge York as his metropolitan see, and it gave Aelred an opportunity of visiting an old friend and talking of things that were nearer to his heart. It must surely have been Waldef, by this time prior of the canons of Kirkham, just north of York, who told him of the wonderful men who had come to England from abroad, all of two years ago now, looking like angels in their white woollen habits, men among whom there were no distinctions save those of holiness, who seemed to have realized the ideal of the apostolic community to be of one mind and heart in love. This was news indeed, and it seemed that a meeting could easily be arranged. Who better than Thurstan could give Aelred an introduction and set him *en route* for Helmsley with a word of encouragement? His business done in York, Aelred rode out to Walter Espec's castle for the night, and the following morning they went to see the monks.

Walter Daniel must have got his facts right when he tells us how Aelred tried to cope with the strength of the attraction a single day's visit to Rievaulx produced in him. It would be like the man we know from his own writings to make the fulfilment of so strong a desire dependent on the will of another, when he asked one of his company, the morning after another night at Helmsley, if he were in favour of a second visit to Rievaulx before they left for home. His affirmative reply was decisive for Aelred and helped to resolve any lingering doubts. Little was now needed to make him decide to stay for good. The party would have to return to Scotland without him, while he, and the one man who wanted to stay with him, spent the statutory four days in the guest-house, before starting the year's noviciate. At this point too a veil of almost complete silence comes down over Aelred's life for several years.

This does not mean, however, that there is nothing trustworthy we can say about it. Only experience could teach one what it means to sing the psalter and the hymns and chants of the liturgical year day after day, and confine's one's reading exclusively to books like the Bible, Cassian's *Conferences*, and the writings of the Fathers, until their words and phrases fill the mind and give shape to the

deliverances of the feeling and imagination. It is nevertheless necessary to suppose how profoundly formative so exclusive a training
must be. But, in addition to this, the normal world of the fervent
monk anywhere, there were things more specific to Rievaulx. When
Aelred began his noviciate the community was still living in temporary wooden buildings down by the river, where they must have
felt the immediacy of the four seasons, like the labourers and lay-
brothers whose lives theirs, at least part of the time, designedly
resembled. Such men it is true by no means always take so conscious a delight in the prospect of trees with their leaves fluttering
gently to earth as Walter Daniel seems to, but it is possible that
Aelred and some of his contemporaries were not so indifferent to
natural beauty as St Bernard is reported to have been. We can be
more certain, from various hints in what he writes later, that
Aelred found, as he had at court, the prospect of his fellows wholly
absorbing and instructive, whether he had occasion to speak to
them or merely observed them moving in silence about their duties
in house or choir. They served him for landscape, and not only did
he make new friendships among them, but from them, especially
from Abbot William and the founder members of the community,
he absorbed that extraordinary homogeneity of outlook which must
have made the Rievaulx Aelred knew so manifestly a daughter of
Clairvaux. It is possible to recapture with reasonable certainty something of both the physical and spiritual atmosphere of the place as
the permanent buildings began to rise and the distinctive life of
the community to take shape.

We must banish from the mind that impression of light and
grace which the present ruined choir, built almost a century after
Aelred's death, creates, and replace it with an image of a church,
now barely more than outlined by low walls, whose eastern end the
new choir transformed. We are fortunate that an almost exact
contemporary and sister of this church, in style and spirit, still survives in the church of the Abbey of Fontenay, the second of the
daughters of Clairvaux, founded in 1118. This church, built at the
expense of Everard, a retired bishop of Norwich who died at Fontenay in the habit, was consecrated in 1147. Rievaulx church, which
almost certainly ante-dates that of Fontenay by two years or more,
had a similar cruciform plan, an identical number of bays in the
nave and, with its plain pointed arches and round-headed windows,
must have presented an appearance as simple and austere as

Fontenay does today. Seldom has the architecture of churches so adequately expressed the ideas of those who built them as these early Cistercian churches did. Their beauty is that of the mind. They are at once the expression of and the natural background to the kind of things St Bernard had been saying to his monks in expounding to them that doctrine of humility which occupies a central place in the Rule of St Benedict. It was at the request of his cousin Godfrey, the founding abbot of Fontenay, that he set some of them down in the first of his treatises, *On the degrees of humility*, written before 1125. To ponder its doctrine is the most sure introduction to the spiritual climate he created for his sons.

To them he offers a life which begins and ends with experience, a recurrent word in his teaching, as it is in that of Aelred after him. Its starting-point is that knowledge of oneself which strips off all pretences and discovers the naked truth, for "humility is the virtue whereby a man recognizes himself as he genuinely is, and so goes down in his own estimation".[55] This is the first step in the return to the living Truth in person. If this way has its hardships, it has its ultimate reward in the complete fulfilment of the soul in love, foretastes of which begin to come in "little morsels"[56] to those who have passed through the initial difficulty of turning from and repenting of the sins they find in themselves. Although this purgation is inevitably something hidden and personal, largely perhaps the fruit of those periods of private prayer which the Cistercian customs will explicitly permit as an alternative way of spending the time allotted to reading,[57] it produces a tangible social result. Among the beatitudes of the Saviour who became incarnate that he might know by experience what he always knew by nature,[58] it is fitting that the beatitude of the meek should come before that of the merciful. For where men are concerned, it is by starting with the knowledge of what I myself am really like that I come to understand other men and have a genuine fellow-feeling for them. This is why the apostle says that those who are spiritual should restore their neighbours in a spirit of gentleness, lest they too should be tempted.[59] It is thus that, in Bernard's scheme, the heart that grows in the love of God grows in the love of its neighbour, and the disposition of compassion is presupposed to the forgetfulness of contemplation, being the special work of the Holy Spirit, "friend and brother".[60] It is this Spirit that, through the growth of the virtues in response to the demands of love in the common life, prepares the soul for those

3

precious moments when as it were "for the space of half an hour", it is lost in the embrace of that love of God which is the complete answer to its deepest desires. There it learns something of Truth's incommunicable secrets, and returns to display them in its life.

This was the school in which, on entering Rievaulx, Aelred felt convinced he could solve his problems and learn the meaning of his life. From about 1135 the masons began to cut the brownish yellow sandstone for the building of the church from a quarry about half a mile away, and the water was diverted to enable the stone to be brought to a point from which it could be conveniently hauled over the last two hundred yards to the chosen site. It is certain that the work was done under the direction of skilled labour,[61] but there was plenty for everyone to do and Aelred, never physically very tough, did not spare himself at it. The work of construction was to go on for perhaps ten years. Aelred would have spent almost as long, since his entry, working at the inner task of his own formation by reading, prayer, and discussion, before he would be required to communicate his vision to other beginners as their novice-master. If the journey to Durham in 1138 marked his re-emergence into the larger world after a long and fruitful period of seclusion, the death of archbishop Thurstan in 1140 led to a commission that took him to Rome and brought him back with something more imperious than a mere suggestion from St Bernard that he should begin to write.

2

A Way of Life

"My monstrous life, my tormented spirit, declare themselves to you", St Bernard once wrote to a Carthusian prior, "I am a sort of contemporary chimaera".[1] It was a telling self-description of the man who, having given himself with a zeal that passed the bounds of discretion to the austerities of an already austere life, now threw himself with equally relentless energy into almost every ecclesiastical dispute of his day. Archbishop Thurstan died on 6 February 1140. In April of the previous year, 1139, the second Lateran Council had by its twenty-eighth canon re-asserted the right of religious communities to a voice in the deliberations of the elective chapters of their neighbouring cathedral canons. It was not long before St Bernard was learning from the Cistercian abbots of Rievaulx and Fountains of their dissatisfaction with what had been happening at York after Thurstan's death. At one stage in the protracted negotiations Aelred's friend Waldef, prior of the canons of Kirkham, had been offered the vacant see in terms he could only reject with horror.[2] When William the treasurer of York was at last chosen in circumstances which seemed to accord with an already unsavoury reputation, Robert Biseth, the prior of the canons of Hexham, displayed the common sympathies of the reformed communities of the North by resigning his office and going at once to St Bernard at Clairvaux.[3] The priors of Kirkham and Gisborough, moreover, decided to make common cause with the abbots of Rievaulx and Fountains and the minority in the cathedral chapter in putting their case to Rome. St Bernard had already been besieging the pope with protests[4] and was desperately anxious to forestall the manoeuvres of the archbishop-elect who, anticipating trouble, had made sure of getting on the road to Rome first. Now, hard on his heels, Aelred of Rievaulx and Walter of London, archdeacon of York, as representatives of the opposition, would be able personally to consult with Bernard and collect letters of introduction to Innocent II and other influential personages at the papal court.[5] Aelred and his companion must have passed through Burgundy about March 1142 and possibly returned by the same route to report on what had happened in Rome. Aelred, it would seem, had created a distinctly favourable impression, though he had to bring back a letter from Innocent summoning the superiors he represented to appear in Rome in the following March in order to make their depositions in the requisite canonical form. The negotiations thus initiated were to be prolonged for many years.[6]

Their details have little direct bearing on the subsequent career of Aelred, but the journey to Rome marks an important stage in his development. It was, in the first place, a sign of confidence on the part of his own abbot William and the other Yorkshire religious superiors that Aelred should have been chosen to represent them on a diplomatic mission of consequence. The position of trust he already held in his own monastery was confirmed on his return by his being given the charge of forming the novices, a task in which his ready insight and his capacity for mild persuasion would be adequately employed. Indeed, it would only be a matter of months before he would be called to fill the post of abbot in the newly-founded daughter house of Revesby in Lincolnshire.

As novice-master Aelred inevitably had to begin to communicate to the young men who were being attracted to Cistercian life in such notable numbers a vision of the meaning of its ideals. Besides solving their personal problems and helping them through their initial difficulties, he had to be able to set before them a picture of the hidden possibilities of monastic life attractive enough to sustain their ascetic efforts and fire their enthusiasm. It was intimate and exacting work, requiring of him, if he responded to its invitation, an ingenious, personal interpretation of all he had been absorbing in his hours of reading, all he had slowly assimilated through his general monastic formation. He may well have hesitated before these demands, being acutely aware, as he was, of his own unsolved problems. For it was at the period when he was in charge of the noviciate that he felt it necessary to take the opportunity of constructing a tank concealed under the floor, in which, like the Celtic saints his ancestors had loved and admired, he could lower himself into the ice-cold waters of the river.[7] Writing some years later to his sister, he describes in an obviously autobiographical passage how he shivered and prayed there for the grace to be able to realize the ideals he had set before himself. It was, perhaps, a young man's way and, considered in relation to his physique, a young man's folly, and it must have played some part in the excruciating maladies he suffered in later life. He would deal with himself and with others with a more large-minded and discerning firmness *then*. But for the time being it was the only way he knew.

It was thus a genuine humility, as much about his personal attainments as about his literary abilities, that made Aelred defer starting on a project St Bernard had most probably formulated for him when they met at Clairvaux in the spring of 1142. For Bernard can scarcely have failed to know how absorbed in the traditional ascetic teaching of the Fathers this modest and intelligent young monk was, and how profitably he was beginning to apply his knowledge to the resolution of his own difficulties. He had reached the point where, in Bernard's judgement, it was time to share more widely the quite special kind of learning which his monastic school among the trees in a Yorkshire valley had given him. A subsequent peremptory letter from Bernard, referring to this or to some previous communication between them, was eventually used by Aelred as part of the justificatory preface to the completed work for which Bernard had asked.[8] It was he who had given it its title and outlined its general plan. It would be a book about Christian love, and was to be called the *Speculum Caritatis*, the *Mirror of Charity*. It would deal with the true nature of charity, its joys and rewards, with the hardships of its contrary, the self-centred love of cupidity, and finally with the delicate art of charity as a way of life. It ought to be an indirect apology for the Cistercian ideal and it was nonsense to suppose Aelred incapable of writing such a book on the plea that, as he said, he only knew about kitchen matters. Bernard probably knew, what Aelred himself confesses in his own preface and expands upon at the end of the work, that records of Aelred's daily meditations already existed in some written form, and that only a word of command was needed to make these take a more permanent shape. Nevertheless, it is difficult to believe that so large a work can have emerged in its finished state during the few months of 1142–3 while Aelred was novice-master as, according to

Walter Daniel, it did. It must be to the substantial draft that Walter Daniel refers.

The evidence of the manuscripts of Aelred's works and our knowledge of the processes of composition among his contemporaries must be borne in mind if we are to envisage the facts correctly. Aelred tells us that when he read the Scriptures he jotted down on wax tablets the thoughts which came.[9] Generations of students had been accustomed to carry such tablets hanging from their belts. Sixty years previously the sketch of the argument of his *Proslogion*, which Anselm had written down in the white heat of discovery, had been found smashed to pieces in this initial stage of composition.[10] Such notes were often preserved in less vulnerable form on *schedulae* or odd scraps of parchment, like those on which for many years Aelred kept an early draft of his work on friendship.[11] Students in the schools and secretaries, official and unofficial, thus kept records of the teaching of notable masters and preachers, which several, like Hugh of St Victor and St Bernard, personally revised and corrected.[12] A small collection of Aelred's sermons survives in what appears to be this stage of composition.[13] Many of these texts, which often appeal to us today for their freshness and clarity, were still not normally considered ready for publication by men who, whatever else they had renounced, had not given up a taste for fine letters. In their final state, works intended for this end were finished and ornamented with the expansions and literary graces which suited the taste of the time.

Most of the surviving manuscripts of Aelred's *Mirror of Charity* give us a text of this type. Their provenance suggests that, unlike the later homilies on Isaiah, the completed work enjoyed only a restrained circulation, reaching little beyond England and a few places in the Low Countries. The Benedictine scholar Dom Wilmart was surprised to discover that not only had no copy survived among the extant manuscripts of Clairvaux, but that the ancient catalogue had no record of there ever having been one there.[14] On the other hand, the most popular compendium of the work survives in a Clairvaux manuscript which must be almost as old as any of the complete text,[15] and a second twelfth-century copy from the same library[16] may suggest that 'a monk of Clairvaux soon made himself responsible for reducing the argument of the *Mirror of Charity* to more manageable proportions. Certainly no modern scholar would share the belief of Aelred's first editor, the seventeenth-century English Jesuit, Richard Gibbon, that this emasculated summary represented the draft stage of the writing.

There is, however, a single manuscript in Oxford which may well supply us with the book at the stage when its substance had at last been determined and there was only the final editing to be done.[17] This manuscript reminds us of those remote preparations for writing to which Aelred himself refers, in so far as its last two leaves give us, not yet inserted into its ultimate position, what looks like the draft of a discussion with an Augustinian canon on differences of view about the obligations of monastic rule.[18] The piece may originally have had some connection with the kind of things that were being said to Waldef who, after going to Rome with the Cistercian abbots in 1143 on the summons of pope Innocent, came back determined to become a Cistercian himself. According to Waldef's biographer, Jocelyn of Furness, it was Aelred's view which in the end prevailed against the opposition from the canons which this decision aroused.[19] If it ultimately turned upon the sense in which a monk ought to interpret one of the most familiar of all Augustine's sayings: *Love, and do what you will*,[20] then the discussion had indeed some relevance to the book Aelred was writing.

This, however, was no more than the coincidence of circumstances. The initial and formative impulses behind the writing of the *Mirror of Charity* are made abundantly clear in Aelred's own preface and in the brief paragraph with which the work concludes.[21] Aelred naturally places obedience first, and it is perhaps true that he would never have attempted so systematically to clarify his thoughts in writing if St Bernard had not given him the occasion to do so. But already his affection for his absent prior Hugh had led to an exchange of reflections on topics of mutual interest and, above all, there was his urgent personal need, long expressed in minor literary efforts, to give articulate form to his problems and reconcile himself to theology and to life. In the event, when all three factors combined under the stimulus of a plan that recalled so many ideas that had impressed him as he lived the life of passing from sermons in chapter to reading in the cloister, and from reading to prayer, the result was a book of formidable dimensions. No one will fail to sympathize with the monks who asked for a more manageable account of what he had to say.

Yet, as an introduction to Aelred's talents as a writer, to the themes that remained the abiding interest of his life, to the kind

of books he read and the world of thought and feeling in which he
habitually moved, nothing more complete exists. Here are his first
experiments in the dialogue form, in the rhetoric of the prayer, the
lament, and the soliloquy, and in quiet succinct argument and
exposition. Here, above all, he presents us with a complete vision of
life, of which he will later enrich many of the details, but which
remains substantially valid for him and which, in its more universal
characteristics, will even appear to be so to many who would find it
hard to imagine what it can have been like to live anywhere so
physically uncomfortable as in a twelfth-century Cistercian
monastery.

A misplaced concern about physical hardship and discomfort is,
in fact, as he understands them, at the heart of the complaints
against the Cistercian reading of the Rule of St Benedict which
Aelred undertakes to rebut in the second part of his treatise. This
part of his work, considered in relation to the discussion with the
canons inserted into the third part,[22] gives us an incomparable introduction to the less familiar aspect of the setting in which Aelred was
writing. St Benedict had declared in the prologue to his Rule that
in his monastery he was seeking to establish "a school of the Lord's
service, in which we hope to ordain nothing that is harsh or a
burden. But if, for some good reason, anything be a little strictly
arranged for the correction of vices and the preservation of charity,
do not on that account run away in dismay from the way of salvation, which cannot fail to be narrow at the beginning." Quoting
these words, without the modifying adjective that applies to the
strictness,[23] Aelred insists that the distinctive feature of the Rule is
the small quantity of ordinary food and drink, the roughness of the
clothing, the trial of the fasts and vigils, the back-breaking daily
work, and other observances which the Rule lays down. He cannot
agree that it can or should be characterized by virtues like patience
and humility, which ought to be features of Christian life anywhere. If, as the protagonists of a more mitigated observance con-
tend, the essence of monastic life consists in virtues which mark a
genuine conversion of life then, he argues, it must at least be agreed
that it consists in virtues and observances taken together. For without the observances there would be nothing to distinguish one form
of religious life from another, or the life of monks from the life of
laymen. The distinction these critics of Cistercian observance should
be making, he feels, is not the one they make between matters of

major and minor importance in the Rule, but rather that which St Benedict himself makes between observance and its purpose, namely the correction of vices and the preservation of charity. Should someone then say: "But why quote the Rule against me? *Love and do what you will*. Let us, then, eat and drink, not because we shall die tomorrow, but because we are full of charity." To this Aelred would reply: "Can a man have charity who does not fulfil the Rule he has freely vowed to keep? How can you love him whom you mock at?" Is he then, it might be asked, condemning traditional dispensations of every kind? Certainly not, he will say, but merely dispensations of a kind which amount to a complete destruction of the Rule and the double purpose for which it exists. Obviously there was room for considerable difference of view about when this situation had arisen, but the early Cistercians were, some would now think, dangerously certain on these matters.

Whatever the dangers of monastic pharisaism inherent in such a position, the argument Aelred presents here is the essence of the primitive Cistercian case, and the kind of idealism it inspired is suggested by the fervent novice who, in a dialogue in the second part of the *Mirror of Charity*, describes to Aelred how the life to which he has come at Rievaulx appears to him. "My food is more sparing now, my clothing rougher, my drink from the spring, sleep on my book or on a mattress, when I should like it in comfort. When sleep would be sweetest to the body, the bell gets me up. We eat our bread in the sweat of our own labour. The command to *mortify your members which are upon earth* is fulfilled in us, and also that other saying: *I am become as a beast before thee.* We go where we are led without arguing. There is no place for self-will; no time for idleness. And yet there are things to delight me. There are never quarrels or strife. There are never the fretful complaints of peasants about hard exactions or the wrongs of the poor. There are no pleas or lawsuits. Everywhere is peace and a wonderful freedom from the noise of the world. Such unity and concord is there among the brethren that everything seems to be everybody's and each has all. No attention is paid to status, no heed given to birth. Only need makes for diversity, only weakness for inequality. For what is produced by the common labour is given to everyone, not according to the dictates of natural sympathy or personal preference, but exactly as each one needs. It amazes me that the will of one man can be the law of three hundred, so that whatever falls from his lips is observed as though all had sworn to do that very thing, or had heard it from God."[24]

This reminder of the size to which the community at Rievaulx had grown in so short a time, and of the quality of the men it had attracted, making the atmosphere there seem so sharply different from the rough and ungrateful character of life in the world at large, is not the only eulogy Aelred puts on the lips of his novice in the final version of this little dialogue. Its concluding sentiments doubtless voice what Aelred, and those of his contemporaries who had been won to the ideals of Cîteaux, genuinely continued to feel. "To say a lot in a little, I find nothing in the evangelical and apostolic precepts of perfection, nothing in the writings of the holy Fathers, nothing in the sayings of the monks of old, which seems to be out of accord with this Order and this profession."[25] On this Aelred makes the comment, which will perhaps have been running through the minds of many who read these enthusiastic and apparently uncritical praises of monastic observance: "You are a novice, and so I attribute what you have said to fervour rather than to vainglory. But I should like you to be on your guard, lest you should suppose that there is in this life any profession that does not have its frauds." It is thus that Aelred reveals, even in this the first of his works, his awareness of the dangers of empty conformism inherent in any boast of fidelity to rule. Of these dangers he probably became increasingly conscious, and there are at least some matters on which one may suspect he later modified the views he had held when he was writing the *Mirror of Charity*. Certainly the occasional tone of unbending sternness scarcely again returns, though the influence from which he derived it remains.

Jerome does not appear to be directly quoted in the *Mirror of Charity* as he sometimes is in later works of Aelred, but his presence is hinted at and can certainly be felt among the holy Fathers who would have approved of life at Rievaulx. The uncompromising nature of Jerome's defence of the monastic ideal, and the ferocity of his tirades against its detractors in his letters and treatises, undoubtedly colours Aelred's style in the second part of the *Mirror of Charity*, where it is those ideals that are being discussed. Jerome's lengthy attack on the otherwise almost unknown Jovinian, whom he calls "the Epicurus of Christianity", is explicitly alluded to by Aelred in this part of his book (ii, 6), and it is clearly under the influence of the section which deals with Jovinian's views on fasting[26] that Aelred characterizes the promoters of more indulgent ways as disciples of the classical physician Hippocrates (ii, 5). Jerome's manner also affects more than one passage in this part of Aelred's book, which is an anatomy of cupidity in its monastic form considered under St John's three headings of lust of the flesh, lust of the eyes, and the pride of life. Under the first of these headings Aelred is concerned with problems more extensive than those created by monks who expect the number of dishes at table to be regulated by the number of lessons read during the Office of the previous night and ask for more succulent meals and rarer seasonings according to the rank of the feast (ii, 4). Here Aelred's satire recalls the objections of the monks who went out from St Mary's, York, to make the foundation at Fountains, but upon it he hangs a prolonged and very personal discussion of fundamental ascetic principles. The mood of Jerome returns with the chapter on elaborations in the chant and eccentricities in its performance (ii, 23), and again with that which treats of the lust of the eyes and the general gratification of the senses (ii, 24). There are monks who keep pets, cranes and greyhounds, does and fawns, and whose houses are gay with coloured pictures and sculptures, their churches spacious and lofty, glowing with candles and precious vessels, the marble floors spread with carpets; men who read Virgil with the Gospels, Horace with the prophets, and delight in Cicero as well as in Paul.[27] The tongue of Bernard himself in the *Apologia* is not more scathing.

If these early Cistercian writers can all affect this style, it is because imaginatively they seem to live in the world of the authorities they cite and to feel them as their contemporaries. Their sense of having the weight of authority behind their views is strengthened by a direct and living contact with their sources. Thus Aelred contrasts the excesses he condemns with the teaching of Augustine, Ambrose, and Gregory, and the example of Anthony and Macarius (ii, 23–4), and he obviously has documented arguments for doing so. That this is the case is the result of the injunction of St Benedict's final chapter that his monks should study the great patristic writers and the lives of the Fathers of the Desert. A twelfth-century volume of lives of these desert Fathers, which once belonged to the Cistercian abbey of Biddlesdon, founded in 1147, is still an eloquent witness to the implementation of Benedict's advice.[28] Its begrimed and frequented pages are convincing evidence of regular use.

Rievaulx certainly lived by the same tradition, and when Aelred talks to Bernard about having come from the kitchens to the desert on entering Rievaulx,[29] the phrase is no mere literary affectation. To both men it would seem that in the houses of Cîteaux the deserts of the early centuries were peopled once again. Occasionally, as at Revesby, which was founded from Rievaulx at the very time when the *Mirror of Charity* was being written, a physical solitude was actually created, even at the expense of destroying three small villages almost without trace.[30] Yet, although this touch of romanticism about the desert was a mark of Cistercian idealism from the beginning, the interior and spiritual significance of the desert, so impressively worked out in the homilies of the great Origen on the wanderings of the children of Israel, was to them more important still. Later in the century Cistercian libraries in England tended to go in for splendid volumes of those homilies of Origen which were known in the Latin translation of Rufinus, but to judge from the appearance of those that survive today these books were reserved for admiration rather than for use, once the first generation of monks was spent. If Origen's influence is present in Aelred, it is more elusive than others that are nearer the surface. Yet the sequence of ideas and images which occurs towards the end of one of the chapters of the second part of the *Mirror of Charity* (ii, 15) is so close to that of Origen's Seventh Homily on Exodus that it is difficult to believe Aelred had not read it. As we accumulate the traces his reading has left upon his work, Origen probably ought not to be forgotten.

Jerome apart, the four great Latin Fathers are undoubtedly textually cited in some form during the course of the *Mirror of Charity*, yet none is unreflectively repeated. All have been transformed by twelfth-century ways of thinking, and reminiscences of them provide a framework in which to express contemporary convictions and answer personal problems. Their wisdom is distilled. Hence it would be foolish, save where direct contact is clear and certain, to take too narrow a view of Aelred's sources, or even to exclude near-contemporary intermediaries. That with their help he reaches an expressive power of his own will be evident from that aspect of the argument of the second part of the *Mirror of Charity* which will probably seem most substantial to the modern reader. It hangs upon problems raised by Cistercian austerity and arises directly out of a view of monastic observance. But it has a wider and more permanent significance for the Christian life in any form and, as such, is a twelfth-century witness to the continuity of a long ascetic tradition.

The fundamental question Aelred is discussing in the second part of the *Mirror of Charity* is that which arises in the minds of those who, like the monks, try to take their Christian life seriously, yet do not seem to find that the Lord's yoke is as light and easy to bear as in the Gospels he promised it would be. Why is this? Reminding the monks that they are, after all, professed to the cross of Christ, he invites them to take the keys of the Word of God and lock themselves in the cloister of their hearts until they discover the roots of their difficulties within themselves (ii, 1). For he is persuaded that these difficulties are radically interior, not simply for the dogmatic reason that the doctrine of original sin sees everyone as suffering from a deep inner disharmony which only grace and the practice of the virtues can cure, but also on account of the ordinary observation that our experience is to a very notable degree determined by our psychological attitude. Thus huntsmen and hawkers will go through any amount of physical hardship in the pursuit of their favourite sport, and yet never feel better than when doing so. Why, then, should it be any less credible when, in a more worthy cause, we are told that the apostles came away from a scourging by the Jews *happy to have been counted worthy to suffer reproach for the name of Jesus*? When do the courses of the adulterer or the thief cause them pain, driven as they are by their different desires? The fact of the matter is that two men can sit down at the same table before the same food, and one find it entirely to his taste, while the other has nothing but complaints. It is evident from innumerable examples that whether what happens to a man brings him peace or trouble is determined simply by his state of mind. Thus, too, when the love of God completely possesses the heart of a man it transforms the character of everything he experiences, not suffering him to be thrown off his balance by any untoward events, but rather turning vicissitudes themselves to his profit. However, this condition of things is, naturally, the goal of the ascetic life, and while the soul is still engaged in the rectification of its desires, while it is still cupidity rather than love which rules it, it is enough for something a little difficult to happen for its unreformed passions to break out like beasts from their lairs and tear it to pieces (ii, 2–3).

This is the reason why those who are looking for spiritual peace need to look carefully into the inner causes of the things that disturb them. *Why do wars and dissensions arise among you,* asks St James, *Do they not arise on account of your desires, which are at war in your members?* The poisonous founts of all these troubles, Aelred believes, are those three forms of perverse love which St John in his first epistle refers to as the lust of the flesh, the lust of the eyes, and the pride of life. Aelred is concerned in the first place to refute "the laughable opinion of those who make spiritual sweetness somehow consist in a pleasant condition of the body, asserting that bodily affliction is contrary to the spirit, and that a man's outward sufferings diminish his inner holiness" (ii, 5). This is perhaps a delibe-rately unfair way of characterizing the point of view of those who, in their need to make a case for dispensations from the hardships of monastic rule, draw attention to that interdependence of mind and body which has come to be one of the axioms of modern medical practice. Yet in seeing that those who are attracted by this approach may be tempted to identify spiritual grace with what is sometimes its physical and psychological effect, and so preach a Christianity without the Cross, Aelred has a worthy and serious point to make. It would be easy to make his position sound a great deal more extreme than it is. In setting his own experience and that of his fellows at Rievaulx against the opinions of their critics, he is careful to assert the two traditional norms of sound asceticism. Voluntary mortifications, he says, must in the first place be directed by a right intention, which excludes their being simply pathological manifestations, and presupposes a genuine call of God weighed in the light of sound reason. Then, further, they should never take the form of private eccentricities, but benefit from the norms arrived at by mature men of experience, so that the discretion which regulates them is not a counterfeit softness, but the true wisdom of the Fathers. Granted this, he feels able to assert with St Paul that spiritual consolation abounds in proportion to outward hardship.

This is the natural point at which to insert an appraisal of "the Athlete of Christ", who tells us so openly of his trials and fears, and to cap it with the clinching text from the Second Epistle to the Corinthians, where he says that *as the sufferings of Christ abound in us; so also by Christ doth our comfort abound.* The words suggest an immediate connection with the closing phrases of the prologue to St Benedict's rule. Who, then, is so foolish, so presumptuous, as to assert against the manifest truth and the apostolic authority that a share in the sufferings of Christ is contrary to the interests of the spirit?

To share in the sufferings of Christ is to be submitted to regular observances, to mortify the flesh by abstinence, vigils, and work, to submit one's will to the judgement of another, to prefer nothing to obedience, and that I may sum up a great deal in a few words, to follow our profession, which is made according to the rule of St Benedict, that is to say, to share in the sufferings of Christ, as our legislator declares when he says: *And so persevering until death in the monastery, we may share by patience in the sufferings of Christ, that we may deserve to be partakers of his kingdom* (ii, 6).

If a case for the austerities of the monastic life, on the basis of scripture and ascetic tradition can be made out, this is it. But it does not solve all the problems Aelred has to confront, for it still does not assess the true place of sensible feeling in such a life. Someone at once observes that when he was better housed and fed, he was often stirred by religious emotion, but now in the monastery he can scarcely, even with an effort, squeeze out a tear. Aelred is not disturbed by this objection, but retorts with the tale of a monk who spent all day yarning and drinking, and returning late at night woke the entire monastery with his sobs of contrition. "Is regular discipline to be forsaken in the hope of compunction of this kind, then? Who would not be horrified at the suggestion?" (ii, 7).

It is clear that visitations of sensible feeling are not in themselves always signs of holiness. They are, in fact, sent by God for different purposes. Sometimes they come as a stimulus to do better, sometimes as a help to bear with a period of special difficulty, sometimes as a foretaste of the joy and peace of holiness achieved. Each stage of the spiritual life has its appropriate graces. The religious feeling which excites fear or love is ambivalent in beginners. Like the gift of tongues or of prophecy, it can be shared by the evil and the reprobate as well as the good. Its misuse turns it into a judgement on the wicked, while it comes as a blessing to the good, in so far as it brings about the reformation of their lives. Those who thus begin to work at the difficult task of their own perfection in the ways of love, avoiding the consolations of frequent chatter and meetings with friends, are sometimes consoled by God himself, who either saves them from falling into their temptations or refreshes them after their struggles, feeding them with frequent tastes of divine sweetness. Yet, since they are still not established on the heights, these graces are only to be interpreted as preparations for holiness rather than its fruits (ii, 8–10).

Few, very few, are raised to that third kind of visitation in which the soul begins to have a foretaste of the firstfruits of its future reward, *going over into the place of the wonderful tabernacle, even to the house of God*, pouring itself out above itself, intoxicated with the nectar of heavenly secrets. Yet this is the path of the soul's destined fulfilment, beginning from fear and finishing with love. The fruit of the graces of the first phase is true conversion to God. At the second stage these graces bring the mortification of self-will and all the passions, at the third, ultimate happiness. Some men get lost at the second stage for want of fidelity, when they have to meet the scandal of the Cross in their own lives, or when they cannot wait for the words *Friend, come up higher*, but as soon as they begin to make a little progress immediately seek *the first seats in the synagogues* (ii, 11–13). If one is seeking for a criterion of one's spiritual progress one must look for it in scripture itself, above all in the memory of what happened to the children of Israel in the desert. "If you have chosen to earn your living, not under the curse of the peasants, but by your own and the common labour of your brethren, if in place of talkativeness you have developed a taste for silence, for fraternal love instead of endless argument, if you have already begun to pay the vows your lips have promised; if, I say, from these and similar signs, you discern that you yourself have come out of Egypt and like a true Israelite, have crossed the great and wide sea, the sea of this world, yet still the manna of heavenly sweetness has not begun to flow for you, do not murmur against God, do not tempt God and say: Is God with us, or not?" (ii, 15). For there are still many labours to be undergone from one's own desires until, after countless struggles, the soul, aflame with heavenly love, is ready to enter the land of promise, and feels at last how easy the Lord's yoke is, how light his burden.

One must not let oneself be easily discouraged because the road is long, and thereby lose the fruits of the good beginning one has made. It is now that Aelred virtually recapitulates what he has been saying by inserting a little dialogue with a novice (ii, 17–20), who has just reached the point of being able to assess both the attractions of the life before him and its solid difficulty. This section makes the occasion for giving a final precision to the sense in which the quest for experience is a legitimate one. For as Aelred now says, and as the whole tenor of his argument has already implied, "experience is deceptive". Augustine confesses his shame at having wept for Dido, and Aelred's novice, perhaps remembering this, recalls that he too has often shed tears over the romances about King Arthur (ii, 17), which may well have been heard as lays before Aelred left the court in Scotland. Tears and strong feelings are thus not in themselves anything by which to set great store. As Aelred concludes, summing up his theory:

> No spiritual man can be ignorant of the fact that our love of God is not to be estimated by these transitory feelings, which are far from being in our control, but rather by the abiding quality of the will itself. To join one's will to the will of God so that the human will consents to whatever the divine will prescribes, there being no other reason why it wants this or that, save that it knows that God wants it; this is what it is to love God. For the very willing is nothing other than love (ii, 18).

It is thus that, in an account of spiritual development which is far from undervaluing the role of feeling and ordinary human incentives, Aelred reaches a position which transcends what can be measured in this way, and shows that what really counts is the one tangible sign which the Church has continued to feel to be the only sure gauge of holiness, the quality of a life lived. As two textual citations indicate,[31] Aelred has in mind Gregory the Great's insistence, in more than one place, that the proof of love is shown in what one does rather than in what one feels, whether that proof be given in patient suffering or in action. Aelred is fully aware that this view has behind it the guarantee of "him who does not lie". *He that hath my commandments and keepeth them; he it is that loveth me*, St John quotes our Lord as saying (ii, 18).

It need scarcely be said that this justification of the monastic calling with its complement of traditional ascetic teaching presupposes a complete doctrine of love for its setting, and this the rest of the *Mirror of Charity* is designed to provide. Just as for Aelred St John is "the one who knows the secrets" (i, 28), and hence in holy scripture it is his gospel and his first epistle that provide Aelred with a point of continuous return, so among the Western doctors it is the "doctor of charity" who has the place of predilection among Aelred's sources, "your Augustine",[32] as Aelred's sons affectionately called him. In his life of Aelred Walter Daniel tells us that Augustine's *Confessions* was among the volumes Aelred had with him when he was dying, since the *Confessions* had been his "initiation into theology, when he was converted from the world".[33] The large perspectives of its closing books are indeed as vital for the theoretical groundwork Aelred has to lay in the first part of his *Mirror of Charity*, as the memorable autobiographical pages of books seven, eight, and ten are for the more personal aspects of what he has to say. A reminiscence of their "late have I loved Thee" appears in an account of Aelred's own conversion which is shot through with such allusions.[34] But the *Confessions* are by no means alone among Aelred's Augustinian equipment in the composition of the *Mirror of Charity*. The sermons on St John's Gospel, if not those on the First Epistle, have certainly played their part, as a verbal citation from one of the most important[35] in the first part of Aelred's book reveals (i, 11). It is from this same twenty-sixth tractate on the gospel that Aelred must have drawn the quotation from Virgil which he uses in the second part[36] to the same purpose as Augustine does in explaining the relation between love and spontaneity, though, close as their common appeal to human experience is, Aelred resists the temptation to adopt Augustine's apostrophe, "Give me a lover and he will understand!" The fidelity of Aelred's discipleship is perhaps the only reaffirmation needed to show that the basis of the sympathy between the two writers is more than an intellectual one. Aelred must constantly have had the impression, as he read Augustine, that the words that would express his own experience were invariably being put into his mouth, so that in the end it was difficult to say to which of the two they belonged.

Yet great as the satisfaction of finding a theory of love so complete must have been, it would never have been adequate had it not extended to the deepest mysteries of faith. It is here that we may be confident of the influence of a work of Augustine to which Aelred remained faithful all his life, perhaps the greatest of Augustine's attempts to write a commentary on the theme of creation as it is described in the book of Genesis. It was this book, the *De Genesi ad litteram*,[37] an exposition of the letter of the book of Genesis, which had much that was relevant to say about what seems to be

the nearest to the statement of a personal plan to be found in the
Mirror of Charity. Bernard had proposed the familiar Augustinian
opposition between charity and cupidity as a framework for discussion, and this had suited Aelred well enough. But he seems to
have shared with many men of that generation a craving for the
resolution of the conflicts and tensions of a world of enlarging experience, so that to him the spiritual significance of the biblical
notion of the sabbath is as fascinating as it was to the tormented
Abelard[38] or the inquiring Hugh of St Victor. It determines, as far
as one can see, Aelred's personal view of the shape of his treatise
and establishes the links between his exploration of scripture and his
patristic reading. He demonstrates that the contemporary method
of collecting what were called *distinctiones*, or distinctive themes
from scripture and the Fathers, could occasionally prove theo-
logically very fruitful. The opening passage of the third part of the
Mirror of Charity suggests that the inner coherence of Aelred's
doctrine of love was clarified in connection with this discipline,
which he believed was actually exemplified in scripture itself. "We
read in the Old Testament", he says, "of certain distinctions of
sabbaths" (iii, 1). He has noticed that the book of Leviticus has
collected a number of different kinds of sabbaths into one chapter.
This is a matter for careful reflection. For, although a mystical
interpretation of the sabbath as such occurs frequently in
Augustine,[39] and in other patristic writers too, none offers a
systematic presentation of the related notions accumulated in this
Old Testament book.

There are very definite indications that it was from brooding
upon Augustine's meditation on the sabbath in the fourth book of
his *De Genesi ad litteram* that Aelred arrived at a valuable, original
insight. At least there appears to be no other patristic or medieval
writer who explores these matters quite in Aelred's way. By push-
ing Augustine's thought a step further in precision, and interpreting
the "rest" of the Christian conception of the sabbath as being the
state of charity in the will in respect of its three principal objects,
self, neighbour, and God, Aelred has discovered a means of making
a fuller investigation of this very rich biblical theme than it would
be easy to find elsewhere. A modern biblical scholar will readily
recognize that the point towards which the Hebrew idea of the
sabbath appears to be moving is one of the central Messianic ideas
of the New Testament, the notion which is rendered by the words

"rest", "peace", and, in St John, "abide".[40] For Aelred the arche-
type of this rest is the love between the Father and the Son which
is spoken of in the Last Supper discourse of St John's Gospel. It is
when he equates the sabbath of rest of God with his divine charity
that Aelred seems to have penetrated to the unifying depths of a
mystery that runs through the two Testaments, and to have reached
a special affinity with his favourite evangelist.

We probably come closest to the origins of his insight in a
meditation in the first part of the *Mirror of Charity* on the verse in
the book of Genesis which reads: "And on the seventh day God
ended his work which he had made; and rested from all his work
which he had done." In these words Aelred finds that God's love is
the all-sufficient reason for the creation and the consummation
towards which it moves.

> A great day is this, a great rest, a great sabbath. O, if you under-
> stood. . . . No evening is ascribed to it, no morning, no end, no
> beginning. So the day of God's resting is not temporal, but eternal.
> You might have thought he was like you, needing to create something
> it would delight him to see or in whose realization he might rest; and
> this is why his rest will not be said to be in any creature. You may
> thus know that he lacks nothing but is all-sufficient to himself, and
> did not create anything to yield to his own need but to satisfy his
> abounding charity. Furthermore, he has created all things that they
> may be; he sustains all things that abide that they may abide, guides
> all things to their appropriate fulfilment. Nor does he do this out of
> necessity but by his gracious will alone. So it is that he stretches from
> end to end mightily by his ever-present, all-powerful majesty; yet he
> disposes all things gently, always untroubled and resting in his utterly
> peaceful charity. It is his changeless eternal rest, his eternal and
> changeless tranquillity, his eternal and changeless sabbath. It is the
> sole reason for his action in creating, ruling, directing, moving, pro-
> moting, completing. Hence most fittingly, where his rest is spoken of,
> the completion of all things is shown forth. For his charity is his will
> and that is his goodness, nor is this anything other than what he is.
> So for him, always to rest in his most sweet charity, in his most
> peaceful will, in his abounding goodness, is to be always what he is
> (i, 19).

There can be no doubt that it is again, though this time more
directly, from the same fourth book of Augustine's work on Genesis
that Aelred derives his analysis of the number six which opens the

succeeding chapter of this section of the *Mirror of Charity*[41] and leads us to the theological heart of the work.

We have said that God's rest is his love. And not without reason. "The Father", he says, "loves the Son and shows him all that he does". And again, "as I have kept my Father's commandments and abide in his love". And the Father himself, "This", he says, "is my beloved Son in whom I am well pleased". This mutual delight of the Father and the Son is a most gracious love, a happy embracing, a blissful charity whereby the Father rests in the Son and the Son in the Father. This one of both, nay rather, in which both are one sweetly, graciously, happily, we call the Holy Spirit, who is believed to have appropriated this name to himself since it is clear that it is common to both (i, 20).

All these considerations separate God from his creatures, since in him love is fulfilled and has nothing to seek. He does not suffer from the hunger and thirst which, in one form or another, is the mark of everything he has made. For if, from this vision of pre-eminent selfgiving, unselfseeking charity in God, we now descend to look closer at the creation, we begin to see that every single thing, from the highest angel to the smallest worm, has about it some reminiscence of the divine charity which is as intimate to it as charity is to the life of God. For all things are by nature so adjusted within themselves and related to each other that nothing can be at peace out of its appointed relation to other things. A stone thrown into the air will fall back to earth, oil will rise to the surface of other liquids, one tree will flourish only on heavy another only on light and sandy soil. Animal needs are more complex, but are still limited to pursuing the satisfaction of the senses (i, 21). Man alone strives higher. He cannot rest in anything less than the divine happiness itself, towards which a certain natural drive[42] for ever urges him on. Since nothing can destroy this desire, of which everyone has interior evidence, there is no rest for man except in attaining beatitude. This is the source of man's misery in so far as, deluded by false appearances, he seeks his bliss where it cannot be found. But it is also the source of his glory as a rational being.

O wonderful creature, lower only than the creator, how do you debase yourself? You love the world? But you are nobler than the world. You wonder at the sun? But you are brighter than the sun. You philosophize about the position of this turning vault of heaven? Yet you are more sublime than heaven. You search into the secret causes of creatures? Yet there is no cause more secret than you. Why, then, pursue fleeting beauty when your own beauty is not dimmed by old age or defiled by poverty, does not fade in sickness or perish even with death? Seek, by all means, seek what you are seeking, but do not seek it there (i, 23).

In this transition from the contemplation of God's charity to the hymn in praise of man who, above all creatures, is deeply imbued with a unique longing which knows no created limits, we discover the dynamism of Aelred's treatise. Aelred's idea that man is driven by a natural urge for the divine happiness, for a good beyond all created good, has a long ancestry, and it is only one of the points in the *Mirror of Charity* at which the world of Plato's *Symposium* becomes again, in rather different guise, unexpectedly real.[43] Aelred's is, naturally, a Platonism mediated by Augustine, but at moments re-felt and re-created with a surprising sureness. Like Augustine, Aelred thinks of love as, in itself, a morally uncommitted force,[44] pre-supposed to that differentiation which makes it deviate into the vicious selfishness of cupidity or rise to the self-giving of true charity. It is simply man's share in the cosmic eros which is the inalienable mark of what it is to be a creature.

The chapters in which Aelred evolves his conception may be taken as a characteristic illustration of the way he uses what he has read and of his independence from it. The master here is Augustine. The stone that falls and the oil that rises lead us to the last book of the *Confessions*,[45] which is another of Augustine's expositions of the work of the six days of creation. But we shall at once be sensible of the different approach of the two writers to the same ideas. Augustine's interest at this point is centred on the life of grace in the soul, which is figured by the operation of the Holy Ghost above the waters. The natural tendencies of the stone and the oil serve as illustrations and reflections of the deep experience of the "weight of love" in man. But Aelred's reading of the passage shifts the emphasis. If one may so put it, in Augustine the universe, that great external treacherous world of opinion, is seen to have something in common with man. In Aelred man is seen to have something in common with the universe. Hence Aelred approaches the essentially scholastic idea, which it would probably be an anachronism to read into Augustine, that there is in man, as in every other creature, a natural force which impels him, even unconsciously, to seek the bliss which is appropriate to him. Simple and undeveloped as it is, this is an objective apprehension of man's central situation in a confident, panoramic view of creation such as the masters in the schools were already beginning to work out. We should compare the sequence of Augustine's chapters nine and ten of the closing book of the *Confessions* with these chapters in Aelred's first part of the *Mirror of Charity*[46] in order to savour the excitement of the twelfth-century discovery of the possibilities of human experience. Where Augustine breaks into the praises of the glorified angels, Aelred takes up the praises of man. Even in his nature man is wonderful because of his capacity for rational love. This is a living humanism akin to that of the dialogues of the young men who gathered about Socrates. It is in the light of these fundamental chapters that we come to understand the significance of the assertion with which the *Mirror of Charity* opens—that to have the opportunity to love God is man's special privilege, coming to him with the gift of his rational nature.

> What is more fitting than that your creature should love you, since it was from you that he received the very possibility of loving you? For irrational and insensible things cannot love you; that is beyond their reach. They have, indeed, their capacities, their distinctive features, their place in the world; not that thereby they are or can be blessed in loving you, but that being by your gift beautiful, good, and fitly disposed, they may promote the glory of those who can be blessed because they are able to love you (i, 1).

The realization of this natural possibility of fulfilment in the shared life of charity, whether with God or with his fellows, is in fact threatened in man's present situation by the universal disintegration of the Fall and the effects of personal sin. This image which Aelred uses to recall this concrete situation in the prayer with which he opens the *Mirror of Charity* is rich with allusions. Its first words are a quotation from the psalms, which can be understood in the Latin to mean, "You have spread out your heavens, O Lord, like a scroll," and Augustine had taken the words in this sense in the final book of his *Confessions*, where he interprets them of the scroll on which the text of holy scripture is written.[47] This sense is certainly not absent from Aelred's mind in so far as it is man's situation, both as he knows it from experience and as it is revealed to be in scripture, that he is about to consider. From this firmament of knowledge a few stars of light shine down in this darkness in which we find ourselves. Here, where if God does not take pity on us we shall die of hunger and thirst, the beasts of the forest prowl about, seeking us as their food. This is a picturesque way of describing man's utter dependence upon the free gift of grace for his healing and fulfilment in a condition where, at any moment, his own disordered passions may tear him to pieces. For, although in his fallen state man has not ceased to be made to the image of God, his likeness has become that of the beasts (i, 4). Aelred thus follows his sources in making a convenient distinction between the image and likeness referred to in the text of Genesis which describes the making of man, so that image refers to man's powers in their natural capacity, and likeness to their present action. Aelred will thus habitually refer to the passions working autonomously as beasts or even as furies.[48]

A close examination of this opening section of the *Mirror of Charity*, in which Aelred establishes his picture of man's natural endowments and supernatural situation, suggests that much of what he has to say has come to him through some contemporary intermediary. It is thus no surprise to find that the Oxford manuscript of the work incorporates a passage from a short treatise of Hugh of St Victor, the great master of the reformed canons in Paris, who died about the time Aelred began his *Mirror of Charity*.[49] This would, however, be insufficient to explain many of the details of Aelred's synthesis. Substantially it is common Augustinian doctrine. Thus, it is fitting that man who is made to the image of God should cleave to his creator. This was originally an adherence of man's three spiritual powers to God, which gave him a share in God's eternity, since he always remembered him, and in his wisdom, since what man knew was without error and in his happiness, since there was no wavering in man's love. Now, as a result of the perverse self-love which brought about the Fall, man only remembers, knows, and loves himself. His memory forgetful of God, his knowledge full of deception, his love self-centred, need healing by God's appointed means (i, 3–4). As a result of the redemptive mediation of Jesus Christ, man's memory can be healed by the witness of holy scripture, his understanding by the mysteries of faith, his love by the daily increase of charity. This is the purpose of flying to a "nest of discipline" such as a monastery provides. There, as it were, "all the ends of the earth can remember themselves and return to God" (i, 5).

Deep down in the memory there is, indeed, a spark of remembrance of God, and this Aelred endeavours to fan to a flame by a brief little argument designed to show that it is folly to say in one's heart, "There is no God". The source of this argument presents an interesting puzzle. Aelred certainly did not derive it from Anselm or from any obvious early scholastic writer. Was it suggested to him by one of Augustine's early philosophical dialogues? There is a passage in the *Contra Academicos*[50] which might explain it, and Aelred's final version of the *Mirror of Charity* undoubtedly associates the scepticism he is refuting with the Academics, who are mentioned by name.

In any case the crucial conversion is that of the will, for we return to God, as Augustine frequently says, "not by the steps our feet take, but by the affection of the soul."[51] The renewal of the image of God within us is not primarily an intellectual process. It consists in opposing the counterweight of charity to the perverse attractions of our own cupidity, in permitting the *compendium* of charity to draw us back to the divine centre from the never-ending circle of self-seeking desire in which the wicked go round like the blind Samson at the millstone (i, 15). Midway between these two opposed impulses, one from grace, the other from our corrupted nature, stands man's faculty of free choice, which grace always respects (i, 10ff). These very Augustinian reflections which see charity as giving man back his true inner freedom, lead by a natural sequence to thoughts of the delights of loving and being loved, and of the sabbath of rest to which Christ invites his followers. The sense of peace and liberation enjoyed by those who begin to wear the light yoke of charity is exemplified by an account of the author's own conversion and that of a young monastic friend, whose death gives a dramatic ending to the first part of the *Mirror of Charity* (i, 28 & 34).

The lament for Simon is an attractive consolatory composition, full of memories of Augustine's sorrows for the deaths of his mother and his friends as these are described in the *Confessions*, but it is neither a literary artifice nor a pure digression. It is a transparently sincere tribute to a friend Aelred had made at the time of his conversion to the monastic life, in whom he felt he had seen the ideal he aspired to, and whose life of self-forgetfulness, in the end "forgetful even of me", contrasted so sharply with those expressions of self-love Aelred is about to analyse in the second part of his treatise. Self-seeking in the monastery, like self-seeking anywhere, whether it leads to the quest for exaggerated physical or spiritual comfort, is always at its most pernicious when it takes the form neither of the lust of the flesh, nor of the lust of the eyes, but of that most radical of all the cupidities, the pride of life which Aelred, following Augustine, sees as characterized by the "desire to dominate". Thriving as it does on a restless curiosity about every-thing and everyone, on envy, detraction and suspicion, "marking and judging everything", nothing is so opposed to the affection and admiration that men like Simon inspire or to the peace and harmony of any society (ii, 25, 26).

It is the social dimensions of charity that Aelred is to consider in the final section of his work, and this he does in relation to the three kinds of sabbaths of which the book of Leviticus speaks. To the sabbath of days he assimilates that inner harmony which results in a man whose unruly and self-destructive passions have become quiescent through the labour of seeking what the objective claims of true love in his own regard require. This prepares him to rejoice with those who rejoice and weep with those who weep, to be weak with the weak and burn with the scandalized, in a word to reach a sabbath of years in the compassionate love of his neighbour (iii, 2–4). There are, inevitably, as many different kinds of claims upon our neighbourly charity as there are different kinds of relationships. These Aelred schematizes into six, along the lines suggested by the father of Western monastic theory, John Cassian, at the beginning of his sixteenth *Conference* which deals with the subject of friend-ship. Aelred will discuss this topic in some detail later, but for the moment he insists that the ties of love which unite us with greater or less intimacy to family, friends, associates, and fellow Christians, and beyond these to Jews and heretics, are pre-eminently displayed in that love

> in which the sum of fraternal charity consists, whereby the Son of God became man, and the likeness of the divine goodness is more fully discovered, as our Saviour says in the Gospel: "Love your enemies; do good to them that hate you; and pray for them that persecute and calumniate you; that you may be the children of your Father who is in heaven" (iii, 4).

This reflection serves exactly to situate the role of the incarnate Christ in Aelred's view of the ascetic formation of the Christian. He has already spoken in the second part of the *Mirror of Charity*

of those who fly to "the maternal breasts of Jesus" in their trials
and difficulties, there to draw the milk of that consolation which
comes from his having entered completely into the human situation
for us (ii, 19), but now Aelred develops further the importance for
our growth in the true love of ourselves and our neighbour of the
fact that "the Word has been made flesh and dwelt among us." In
our devotion to the flesh of our Saviour we can, as it were, find an
outlet for our feelings and emotions which actually restores their
innocence. Entering into the scenes of his life as vividly as if we
were present at them, we can spontaneously react with our whole
being to him who became man that we might, as St John insists,
see and touch him, and hence express our affection for him in an
ordinary human way. This is a complete *ascesis* in itself. As Aelred
says, "that a man may not succumb to carnal concupiscence, let
him turn his whole affection to the attractions of the Lord's flesh"
(iii, 5). Language of this kind, and its consequences for the life of
devotion, which will be more elaborately developed by Aelred in
other and later works, has been found with increasing frequency
from the time when Anselm, half a century earlier, in a prayer to
St Paul found himself addressing the apostle, in words suggested
by his own epistles, as "nurse and mother", and passing on to
speak to our Lord himself in similar terms. Now such thoughts
have come to stay and are entering the mainstream of popular
piety.

Here, in the *Mirror of Charity*, this passage on the Incarnation
has the additional function of showing how the three sabbaths of
charity, with ourselves, with our neighbour, and with God, are
interrelated, and how the charity which animates them also inter-
penetrates them. For it is through the consummation of our neighbourly charity in our devotion to the incarnate Christ that we pass
on to the fullness of the spirit in the sabbath of sabbaths which is
union with God himself. Here and elsewhere in his works, Aelred
habitually gives a technical significance to a phrase of scripture
which he uses to refer to this stage of development when the virtues
of Christ are at last shown forth in his disciple. "Before this *the
Spirit was not yet given, because Jesus was not yet glorified*" (iii, 6).

Now that the elements in his vision of the inner life are all in
place, Aelred has the delicate task of distinguishing between good
and bad loves in practice and the embarrassment of facing the
obscurities of the theologians and philosophers behind him on this

subject. We shall at once notice his consistency with the derogatory
terms in which he has referred to those who read Cicero with Paul
in the second book of the *Mirror of Charity*. He is going to talk
about friendship, but he is determined to do so at least without
Cicero's direct help. More than fifteen years later, in the preface
to his own Christianization of Cicero's treatise on this subject, in
which so much of Cicero survives, Aelred tells us what his attitude
had been at the time of his entering monastic life, and his words
seem to be verified in the third part of the *Mirror of Charity*. If
Cicero is present, he is present through other sources, through
Cassian's *Conference* on friendship and through Ambrose's work
De Officiis Ministrorum, On the Duties of the Clergy, an adaptation
of a work of Cicero written while Ambrose was still a compara-
tively new convert to Christianity. In addition, Aelred certainly has
in mind throughout this final section of his work Augustine's great
discussion of relative loves in his *De Doctrina Christiana, On
Christian Teaching*, a book whose influence on the Christian theory
of love in the West is incalculable. It is Augustine's distinction between "using" and "enjoying" created things that will be of special
concern to Aelred. To enjoy, Augustine says, is to cleave with love
to something for its own sake. To use, however, is to refer the
object of use to the obtaining of what one loves.[52] As a means of distinguishing between the creator, in whom alone is true joy, and all
created things, this distinction may sound all very well while it is
being applied to things that are obviously pure means to an end.
But what of our fellow men, all of whom are created beings?
Augustine does not evade this difficulty and from the subtle discussion in which he reaches the conclusion that "no one ought to
enjoy even himself for his own sake, but for the sake of him who
is the true object of enjoyment",[53] Aelred culls a quotation from
scripture which he will use to mitigate the full force of the view
that it is only in God that we can have fruition.

On the way to this, however, there are one or two passages
characteristic of Aelred's lively appreciation of the value of other
human beings. "Doubtless, he says, the happiness of beatitude itself
will be the greater if what a less gifted man cannot have in himself
he begins to have in another" (iii, 9). One is aware how clearly he
sees the people he lives with.

Let us set before us two men, one of whom is gentle, charming, calm,
pleasant, fit for good company, open to communication, sweet-

tongued, urbane, yet less advanced in some of the virtues. The other, although more mature in virtue, has a less happy face, a sterner expression, a countenance marked by his severe habits. He is kind to everyone, gives what is asked of him, yet his company is not enjoyable, nor does his kindness attract others (iii, 18).

These are the kind of observations which objectivity in love presupposes, if the claims of reason and affection are each to be given their proper place

With a few, experience shows that both claims may go together and these are suited to the intimacies of friendship. Aelred has not failed to observe that St Paul, cited by Augustine in his honesty, expresses the wish to "enjoy" Philemon in the Lord.[54] Aelred quotes the text twice as he moves towards the climax of his exposition. That, when it comes, provides us with an interesting measure of the difference between Aelred and his sources. Cicero had said:

What is pleasanter than to have someone to whom you can speak about everything as you would to yourself? How can you have as much joy when things go well, unless you have someone to be as happy about them as you are? Adversity would indeed be hard to bear, without someone to whom it would be harder even than it would to you.[55]

Ambrose, on whom Aelred certainly depends, adapts these phrases thus:

Preserve, then, my sons, the friendship you have entered into with your brethren. Nothing is lovelier in the world of men. It is indeed a consolation in this life to have someone to whom to open your heart, with whom you can share your secrets, to whom you can commit the privacy of your mind, a consolation to choose for yourself a faithful man to congratulate you when things go well, sympathize in your sadness, encourage you under opposition.[56]

Aelred finally produces:

It is no small consolation in this life to have someone you can unite with you in an intimate affection and the embrace of a holy love, someone in whom your spirit can rest, to whom you can pour out your soul, to whose pleasant exchanges, as to soothing songs, you can fly in sorrow, to the dear breast of whose friendship, amidst the many troubles of the world, you can safely retire, to whose loving heart, as to yourself, you can unhesitatingly commit the stomach of all your thoughts; with whose spiritual kisses, as with remedial salves, you may draw out all the weariness of your restless anxieties. A man who can shed tears with you in your worries, be happy with you when things go well, search out with you the answers to your problems, whom with the ties of charity you can lead into the depths of your heart; a man who, though he be absent in body, is yet present in spirit, where heart to heart you can talk to him, all the more delightfully for being so secret, where heart to heart you can confer with him and, when the noise of the world is still, rest heart to heart with him in the sleep of peace, in the embrace of charity, in the kiss of unity, where the sweetness of the Spirit flows between you, where you so join yourself and cleave to him that soul mingles with soul and two become one.[57]

This is romantic love utterly unashamed. In the context, the Augustinian reserves are not denied, but room is made for something quite new and contemporary. Consequently even what is most traditional in Aelred's approach looks rather different. Thus too, with so little resource in the way of classical philosophical literature, using a phrase he perhaps picked up in Jerome,[58] Aelred returns to something like the language of the *Symposium*, overlaid though it be with the new tones of romance. For the phrase translated as "heart to heart", is the phrase that in the neo-Platonic tradition has become "alone to the alone",[59] having travelled far since Alcibiades described to the delighted supper-party how he had tried to get Socrates on his own and all to himself.[60] But then Aelred's book is theology and reflection at work in the service of life and experience and to that extent nearer to what the Greeks of classical times would have regarded as "philosophy" than many of the activities that have gone by that name since the close of the Middle Ages.

Aelred himself can have found little leisure to taste the fruits of the peace he described and aspired to, before he was overtaken by new commitments.

3

Pastoral Charge

The early Cistercian houses, Rievaulx in England among them, witnessed an astonishing regeneration of the monastic tradition. They sprang fresh from an old trunk that had been pruned hard. Aelred had received his monastic training in a community that attracted others as it had attracted him. All his early maturity was passed in an atmosphere of growth and expansion. When it was time for him to speak and to write, he did so under the stimulus of eager and attentive audiences. The support of their ready and intelligent interest makes itself felt in almost everything he wrote on the monastic life. An inner circle of those who were closer to him in sympathy or abilities gradually begins to form itself in the mind from stray allusions up and down his pages, but beyond these are the ever-increasing numbers of those who wanted some share in the secret that seemed to make "the mountains drip sweet wine, the hills flow with milk and honey and the valleys abound in corn"[1] in those days.

Aelred's own novice-master, Simon, had probably been among the first to leave with a founding party, when Walter Espec gave Rievaulx a property in a clearing on his Bedfordshire estates in 1135. In 1136, while regular life was being established at Wardon, a second party went north to Scotland, where king David had given them land at Melrose, a little higher up the Tweed than the former house of that name, in which centuries earlier Cuthbert had become a monk.[2] At the time when Aelred was training his novices and working on the *Mirror of Charity* the complement of the mother house at Rievaulx could be put at the round figure of three hundred,[3] and the moment for another new foundation was already at

Map to illustrate places connected with Aelred's life and journeys. Daughter-houses of Rievaulx, of his period, are shown linked with the founding house.

hand. It was thus that, after only a few months as novice-master, Aelred found himself appointed first abbot of Revesby in Lincolnshire, founded by William de Roumare in 1143.[4]

There is an intimate connection between Aelred's qualities as a writer and those which fitted him for the guidance and government of men. Walter Daniel's estimate of these carries the conviction of a judicious admirer. As one who himself always remained conscious of having been through the discipline of the schools, he saw in Aelred the often enviable gifts of the successfully self-taught man. He insists upon the directness and integrity of Aelred's thought and speech. Yet it had the sophistication which comes from a refined and natural sense of the appropriate. In choosing the metaphor of touch to describe the way Aelred had picked up what he knew, he hits upon the traditional mark of a man of notable intelligence. Intuition was Aelred's special endowment. It was this which gave him an unusually prompt understanding of very different types of men. Everyone wanted his advice or his company. Gifts and favours poured in and, with them, new commitments and new responsibilities. The bishop asked him to preach at local synods and assist in the reform of the clergy, so that soon his paternal concern extended far beyond the bounds of his monastery. His generosity was quite equal to these demands, but sometimes echoes of their repercussions upon his burdened spirit begin to make themselves heard.

The pastoral charge of the abbacy alone was inevitably always present, and it was to be with him, first at Revesby and afterwards at Rievaulx, for the rest of his life. One All Saints' Day, preaching to his brethren, we find him saying:

The Apostle says of everyone without distinction that "all who will live godly in Christ shall suffer persecution". That man lives "godly" who can genuinely say, "Who is weak, and I am not weak? Who is scandalized, and I am not on fire?" As we find by frequent experience, brethren, it is "a great persecution" to know the weaknesses, the sorrows and the burdens of many. It is "a great persecution" to have charge of everyone, to suffer for everyone, to be sad when someone is sad, and fearful when he is tempted. It is, indeed, a still more unbearable "persecution" when, as sometimes happens to us, one of those whom we foster and protect and love with our very entrails is so far overcome by the devil that he actually leaves us, or lives so perversely and God-forsakenly that we are forced to turn him out.[5]

5

Aelred must have taken this final step with very few, but many were the hours of prayer and patient persuasion he devoted to the cases of those whose self-destructive instability would perhaps have ruined them in any way of life. Walter Daniel cites only one example which, from all he says, must stand for many less notorious.[6] Aelred's connection with the monk in question began when the man, a secular clerk already, entered the noviciate at Rievaulx. It requires the intervention of nothing particularly miraculous to believe that on at least three distinct occasions, first at Rievaulx, then at Revesby, and finally back at Rievaulx again, this man was providentially prevented from leaving the only setting in which his spiritual needs would have been properly understood. If he died, in the end, in Aelred's arms, it was a triumph of the faith and pastoral fidelity of many apparently unrewarding years. Walter Daniel, looking at all this in an entirely traditional perspective, sees Aelred in his new position as committed to that exalted proof of love which consists in a willingness to pass, without considerations of personal preference, from the disengagement of contemplation to involvement in activity, thereby developing the virtues of both the one and the other.[7]

Where these survive in some recorded form, the instructions Aelred gave his monks at the different seasons of the Church's year and on the festival days show us how he himself habitually explained the theory of the monastic vocation and envisaged his own role as abbot in relation to it. Although these instructions abound in vivid personal touches and turns of phrase, they show unmistakably that he had what he somewhere calls "a churchman's soul"[8] in his sensitiveness to the abiding relevance of traditional ascetic doctrine. In his hands this tradition comes to life as a practical expression and formulation of the teaching of the Gospels. He speaks as a monk to monks, but with an authentically evangelical voice.

Thus, in a sermon for Christmas day,[9] when it was natural to think of the festivities being celebrated by Christians everywhere, Aelred sets out to explain the monastic vocation against the background of the Christian life in general. "It is rightly my duty to commend to your love today the news which the angel proclaims to the world. Already a decree has gone out from God our emperor that all the world should be enrolled." Just as the earthly emperor at the time of the birth of Christ wanted the whole world to be enrolled so that it should be aware of its relation to the metropolis of Rome, and pay the tribute which bore the emperor's image, so our emperor wishes us all to be enrolled in that free city which is above, the mother of us all. The Christian calling is like this imperial summons, and each of us answers it by going to the city of his own vocation, whether it be to marriage, to the solitude of the desert, to the common life of the cloister or to some other ascetic retreat, there to pay the common tribute, the soul on which God's image is impressed. "Happy is the man who renders him this tribute, who pays him this coin, who gives him back his image." Inherent, then, in this doctrine is the notion that the common Christian vocation is essentially a fulfilment of man's spiritual capacities in a manner which is personal to each one. "For one is the glory of the sun, another the glory of the moon, another that of the stars. And star differs from star in glory."[10] No one was more appreciative of these enduring individual differences, even within a common form of life, than Aelred was.

For him, St Benedict, whose rule the monks follow, is like another Moses, who leads his disciples out of the world as Moses led the Israelites out of Egypt towards the land of promise.[11] This separation from the world for which the cloister provides is, of its nature, primarily that interior separation from unchristian ways of acting and thinking on which all the New Testament writings insist, and it cannot be an escape from the human situation. It is precisely for men in the complexity of their total human needs that the rule explicitly provides. Aelred sees these provisions as grouped under bodily and spiritual activities.[12] The physical asceticism of the rule, its watches and its fasts, is a refuge to those who are still troubled by bodily passions. It gives them the discipline that will make the earth of their bodies fruitful in the practice of the virtues. But the virtues are only for the fullness of life to which they lead, and this is achieved and lived in and through the spiritual activities of reading, prayer, and meditation. It is in those that the monk tastes how sweet the Lord is and begins to enter the land of promise.

The notion that asceticism and the practice of the virtues must fall into place first in point of time in the development of the spiritual man is characteristic of the teaching of John Cassian, who always has his eye on the life of contemplative solitude as the ultimate goal. Aelred, the technical turn of whose language implies the necessary reserves about authentic eremitical vocations, displays no enthusiasm for those who withdraw "on their own initiative" to some wood or kindred place and "eat when they like, sleep when they like, work and rest when they like".[13] He prefers the common life under rule, not only because it involves the intimate sacrifice of one's own will, but also because it provides the objective assurance of a balance which is appropriate to man's present situation. The traditional doctrine of an alternation between action and contemplation corresponds to man's natural psychological needs, and it is for these that he believes St Benedict's rule wisely provides. He is explicit on this point in the longest of his sermons on these themes, preached on a text from the gospel read at Mass on the feast of the Assumption of our Lady:

> In this wretched and laborious life, brethren, Martha must of necessity be in our house; that is to say, our soul has to be concerned with bodily actions. As long as we need to eat and drink, we shall need to tame our flesh with watching, fasting, and work. This is Martha's role. But in our souls there ought also to be Mary, that is, spiritual activity. For we should not always give ourselves to bodily efforts, but sometimes be still and see how lovely, how sweet the Lord is, sitting at the feet of Jesus and hearing his word. You should in no wise neglect Mary for Martha; or again Martha for Mary. For, if you neglect Martha, who will feed Jesus? If you neglect Mary, what use is it for Jesus to come to your house, when you taste nothing of his sweetness.
>
> Realize, brethren, that never in this life should these two women be separated. When the time comes that Jesus is no longer poor, or hungry, or thirsty, and can no longer be tempted, then Mary alone, that is, spiritual activity, will take over the whole house of our soul. This St Benedict, or rather the Holy Spirit in St Benedict, saw. This is why he did not confine himself to saying and laying it down that we should be occupied with reading like Mary, while passing over work such as Martha does; but recommended both to us, and set aside definite times for the work of Martha, and definite times for that of Mary.[14]

This passage, which explains the relation between the observances of rule and the inner reality of a complete life lived with and for God, is thoroughly Augustinian in its conviction that a life of contemplation alone is only possible in the next world. Yet it also implies a specifically Christian vision of the role of other people in the contemplative life as lived in this world, such as St Benedict too insists upon when he tells his monks to see Christ in their abbot, in the sick, in the visitors,[15] in fact in all the daily calls upon their time and sympathy. Without this vision to foster a true sense of the inner meaning of its austerities, the monastic life perishes. Aelred is only too well aware that, if the monastery is rather like a ship at sea, it has to weather a storm of contrary winds and temptations. There is the voice which says:

> How long will you be able to put up with all this? And you still have a long time to live, and always in this distress, always your flesh, your thoughts to fight against, never to be without fear. And, after thirty years of it, you may lose all these labours by a single sin.

"Imaginings and lies"[16] like these, emptying the monk's life of vigour and joy are, however, by no means the most insidious. Those who are given various offices in the monastery to look after, the *obedientiales* as they are called, are perhaps fortunate in having to "provide good things not only before God, but also before men, that in all things God may be glorified".[17] For often those who are free of these responsibilities, the *claustrales*, are also free to preen themselves on their own perfections saying: "O, if I were abbot, or prior, or cellarer, or porter! I should not get mixed up with wordly things. I should do this or that. And in such things they spend almost all their time." On the other hand, according to temperament, there are others who

> "being slack themselves, are not much troubled about anyone else, but since they are free from external cares, give themselves to leisure and ease; and, unable to do so in the body, in their minds go around amid worldly desires and carnal delights, and do not worry about anything as long as they remain in the monastery in body alone."

The monastery is not a place for this kind of pharisaical self-deception or moral evasion.

> For he who in this life is not in the army of the spirit, should not be called a man, but a beast. Since, if he does not fight against the passions and desires of the flesh, but consents to them, he does not live like a man but like a beast. You must know, brethren, that from the day you came here and began to serve Christ, you entered a battle-ground. This is why Salomon says: "Son, when you come to the service of God, stand firm and prepare your soul for temptation". This is the fight. So be strong in battle.

Aelred, indeed, does not mince his words to those who forget all this.

We ought to remember what we are called to. We ought to realize that the men of this world give us their lands and their substance that they may be protected by our prayers and reconciled to God. This is why we have a duty to be their betters in purity of life and the practice of good works, lest it should be said of us: "Blush Sidon, says the sea". Which doubtless happens when those who are called religious are worse than those who live in the world. For then, compared to the sea of the world, Sidon, that is religion, blushes.

Although arguments like these seem to suppose a functional view of monasticism in society, their stress on the primacy of genuine holiness is valid in any social setting. Nor is Aelred's view of what the monastery ought to be incompatible with an entirely merciful attitude towards those defects in its subjects which result from sheer moral weakness, rather than neglect or self-indulgence. A monastery can expect to provide a refuge for some who are spiritually crippled and in a condition rather like that poor man whom the Acts of the Apostles describe as healed by Peter and John as they went up into the temple to pray.

Alas, poor Mephibosheth who, lame in both feet, cannot manage to go up to the delights of contemplation, and even in active good works is backward and remiss. But there is hope if he is carried, if he is placed at the gate of the temple, if he begs alms of those who are going into the temple. Look, my brethren, if there be such men among you, be patient with them, have compassion on them, console them, "instruct such a one in the spirit of meekness", that what the Apostle says may be fulfilled in you: "Bear ye one another's burdens, and so you shall fulfill the law of Christ". And here am I, lame from my mother's womb, "conceived in iniquities and in sin did my mother conceive me", carried by you, by your patience, carried by your advice and your prayers. I have at least made this degree of progress that I am already sitting at the temple gate which is called Beautiful, asking alms from those who are going into the temple.[18]

It is in considerations of this kind that Aelred's own pastoral approach is rooted. It begins in an honest, mutual awareness of spiritual need. The very purpose of the common life under rule is to awaken this awareness and see that its implications are translated into action.

It is certain that by true obedience we arrive at the love of God and our neighbour more easily, as it is written: "You are my friends if you do the things that I command you." This, then, is what the love of God consists in: the love of our neighbour. It is also written: "This is my commandment that you love one another as I have loved you". What more desirable, what more delightful than these commandments of the Lord, on which all the law and prophets depend! And how did the Lord love us? "Greater love than this no man has, that a man lay down his life for his friends." And how will you lay down your life for me, if you will not lend me a needle and thread when I need it? How will you shed your blood for me, if you think it beneath you to give me a cup of cold water, if you cannot be bothered to take your hand out of your pocket for me? If you refuse to say a good word of or for me, when will you die for me? Clearly from these little signs we can discern what progress we are making in obedience, and how far we are from that love of God and our neighbour, on which the whole law and prophets depend. Let us, therefore, obey each other, love each other, for love is the fulfilling of the law. This is why there is as much difference between a living man and a dead body as there is between him who loves and him who does not love.[19]

This earnest Johannine development, which manifestly has in mind some of the less romantic aspects of community living, must be connected with a complementary picture of the inter-dependence of those who live a life in which the talents of each differ.

"Each has his own special gift from God; one in this way and another in that." One offers more work, another is better at watching, another at fasting, another at prayer, another at reading or meditation. Let there be, then, one tabernacle of all the offerings so that, as our legis-lator commands, no one may say or presume anything to be his own, but everything may be for the common good of all. Which is not to be understood, brethren, simply of the cowl and the tunic, but much more of the virtues and spiritual gifts. So let no one take exceptional pride in any gift God has given him, as though it were his own. Let no one envy his brother a grace, as though it were his personal pre-rogative; but let him consider that what is his belongs to all his brethren, nor doubt that what his brother has is also his. For almighty God could make whoever he pleased perfect in an instant, and give to each one all the virtues; but by a kindly economy he arranges that each needs the other and that what he lacks in himself he may possess in another. Thus is humility safeguarded, love increased, and unity made evident.[20]

It need scarcely be said that just as the ascetic observance of rule, the "active life" in its organized form, is pointless and dead without its loving, contemplative centre, so the ideals of community living cannot be attained unless they proceed from the heart, and nothing moves the heart like the remembrance of one's own need and the experience of one's own weakness.[21]

But there are many who have honey in the mouth, yet not dripping from the honey-comb, for many have sweet words, though they do not come from a plenitude of inner sweetness. These men are somewhat like the bee, which possesses both sweetness and a sting. On the one hand they have honey, since their talk is sweet, they charm everyone, do everyone's bidding, but only in what appears. For in their depths, or in their hearts, if you will, those whom they have outwardly anointed with honey, they sting with detraction and rash judgment within . . . And that we may know whence sweetness in words comes, holy scripture at once adds: "Honey and milk are under thy tongue". Anyone who wishes to have that holy sweetness in words which is pleasing to God must keep two considerations in his thoughts and in his heart, holiness as a standard for himself and compassion towards his neighbour. The man who has these in his heart, who concentrates on these, his words will be full of spiritual sweetness. As honey is made from many flowers, so all holiness is made up of many virtues. Thus, by "honey", we might understand "holiness". "Milk", since it is the sign of motherly love and feeds little children, and moves a mother's feelings towards her child, by "milk", we might understand "compassion". Nothing makes a man speak to another tenderly, kindly, and gently, like compassion, though compassion without holiness is moral softness.[22]

These picturesque ways of using the language and images of scripture to expound the ideals of monastic living do not detract from the seriousness and appositeness of their purpose, or conceal the fact that the man who employs them has himself first learned their meaning by practising what he preaches. It is thus no surprise to find him saying that there is a very real sense in which every member of the community has a pastoral duty, whether he be abbot or not.

A man falsely declares he loves God, when he will not feed his sheep. But someone will say: What has that to do with us? This is a matter for bishops, abbots, priests, who have the cure of souls. It is true, brethren, that this is a matter for them, but also for you. The sheep of Christ are fed in two ways, by word and example. I admit, brethren, that there are many prelates in the Church who can adequately feed Christ's sheep by word but, since they live badly, would feed them better if they kept silence, or simply went away and so gave them an example of humility, poverty, abstinence, chastity, and the other virtues. Better still is the man who does both; and anyone who cannot do both would do better to feed the sheep by example than by word.... Our Lord also has his sheep in every soul, that is to say, the virtues, which everyone who loves Christ must feed. These sheep are charity, humility, spiritual joy, and the like. We feed these sheep when we do the kind of things which make these virtues grow in us. But every one of us should also foster these virtues in his neighbour. And we do this when we so live in the sight of our brethren that their charity, their joy, their humility, their patience, grows by our example.[23]

There were many who had their eyes on the man who said things like this. Perhaps he did not always say them so memorably as some of these passages may suggest, for we have only a fraction of the sermons he must have preached, and these presumably among the best, but the influence of his example had already won him a place in the affections of many of his brethren that would determine the rest of his career. According to the Melrose Chronicle,[24] William, the first abbot of Rievaulx, and the abbey's closest link with St Bernard, died in 1145. His memory was to live on among his brethren, who eventually made a shrine for his body in the wall of their chapter-room, where they might venerate him. Such men are difficult to replace, and it was perhaps natural that the successor elected should be probably the most distinguished man in the house, Maurice, a former monk of Durham, whose learning had earned him the reputation of being second in eminence only to Bede.[25] His was not, however, a career or a reputation which suggests any special capacity to care for a community of men as varied and vigorous as Rievaulx seems at that moment to have been, and within two years he had resigned an office which had proved only a bewilderment and a burden to him. It was now, probably in the autumn of 1147, that Aelred was chosen to take his place.

The defence of Aelred into which Walter Daniel launches when he announces this fact is not likely to be an aberration on the part of the biographer, and in any case makes very good sense in relation to a personality as subtle as Aelred's was. For all the evidence suggests that he was indeed the kind of man who establishes a fascination and a power over other men, even by the briefest of contacts and, the more difficult such a power is to define or explain, the more open it is to a sinister interpretation. That simple integrity

really explained everything was something Aelred's detractors in
the monastery would never allow, for as Walter Daniel says,
"goodness is the kind of thing that never fails to excite jealousy".
Throughout the remaining years of his life, even when he lay
twisted with pain in his long final illness, Aelred had to endure the
bitter irritation and criticism his apparently obstinate kindness
aroused in those who could not understand him.

Nevertheless, it is necessary to recognize that Aelred's critics may
sometimes have had a plausible case. Those who have seldom in
their lives known a day's illness or a moment's indecision before the
complex realities of a moral situation commonly find it difficult to
understand that it requires a peculiarly searching form of courage
to live virtuously with many bodily and moral infirmities. Walter
Daniel's contention that Aelred, "the friend and physician of the
sick", had a thoroughly virile attitude towards both his own
physical ailments and the moral imperfections of the spiritually
immature, would only be intelligible to those who could share
Aelred's own insight into these matters. It is not in his wonderful
Pastoral Prayer alone that Aelred is bold enough to place his own
weaknesses of every sort in the context of divine providence over
his own life and that of his subjects. It is as though these very
weaknesses plunged him into the heart of the mystery of what God
is doing in the world. There is, for instance, an Advent sermon
about the vision in which the prophet Isaiah sees God seated on a
high throne . . . "and all the earth was full of his glory".

O time to be longed-for, acceptable time, time that every holy man
desires daily when he asks in his prayer: "Thy kingdom come, thy
will be done on earth as it is in heaven." "All the earth was full of
his glory." The earth I walk, I can see; I am aware of the earth
I bear with me. There is trouble for both, sighing for both, the anger
rather than the glory of God over both. Still the prince of this world
reigns over the children of wrath. Daily he rises up against those who
believe, and there is scarcely one of the holy ones who does not
experience his attacks. Yet "all the earth was full of his glory". And
I know that this earth I walk will be delivered from the servitude of
corruption, and there will be a new heaven and a new earth, and he
who sits on the throne will say: "Behold I make all things new". The
earth I bear with me, too, will be full of the glory of the Lord, though
now my earth cries out against me and the flesh lusts against the
spirit. "Why are you sad, O my soul, and why do you trouble me?"
"Hope in God", for all the earth will be full of his glory. For the

present the earth, cursed in the work of Adam, brings me forth thorns and thistles. It is weak and feeble, reluctant and burdensome, subject to so many passions, exposed to so many sicknesses. But "why are you sad, O my soul, and why do you trouble me. All the earth was full of his glory." And when shall this be? When he sits on his throne high and exalted and changes our lowly bodies to be like his glorious body, when that glory which appeared in the Lord's body transfigured on the mount, also appears in our earth, endowed after the resurrection with everlasting life. . . . Heaven and earth, the sea and all that is in them, every being, every choice, every movement, every affection, every work, every suffering, every honour, every consolation, every persecution will promote the glory of God, and all things will work together for good to his holy ones. Consider, I beg you, what that joy will be, what singing there will be in our hearts when in God himself we see the causes and reasons for everything that is and will be.[26]

Such convictions are all very well for a man of vision who remains spiritually responsive to the changing demands of every passing moment, but it is easy to see how, as the years went on, and particularly during the last ten years of his abbacy, when the Cistercian General Chapter allowed Aelred a wide measure of discretion about his mode of life, the abbot's unpredictable public appearances and withdrawals, recoveries and prostrations, often excited unfavourable comment on the part of those whose horizons were bounded by an exacting daily routine of work and liturgy. Doubtless a graver cause of complaint in a less flourishing and less soundly guided community might have been the administrative policy that went with this doctrine of the primacy of the mysteries of the spirit. For Aelred did not have one law for himself and another for his brethren. From the beginning he set out to make Rievaulx spiritually strong enough to be able to carry the kind of men who would not have fitted in anywhere else, and to make it his boast that "this is the supreme and special glory of the house of Rievaulx that it knows better than any other how to bear with the weak and have compassion on the needs of others."

All [Walter Daniel reports him as saying] weak and strong alike, ought to find in Rievaulx a haven of peace and there, like fish in the wide sea, enjoy the refreshing, glad, and spacious quiet of charity, so that it may be said of her: "Thither the tribes go up, the tribes of the Lord: the testimony of Israel, to praise the name of the Lord." Tribes, indeed, of the strong, and tribes of the weak. For it cannot be supposed that a house which refuses to condescend to the weak is genuinely religious. "Thy eyes did see my imperfect being, and in thy book all shall be written." [27]

The quotation from the psalms with which these remarks are capped is taken from verses which describe how God sees the psalmist while his infant body is still quickening in his mother's womb, and they suggest God's intimate knowledge of and care for each soul.[28] Aelred's use of them is an apt indication of the theological foundations of his pastoral principles and, by implication, of the importance he will attach in his government to fostering in each soul a personal awareness of its relations with God in the hidden recesses of its conscience. Yet there are no signs that these preoccupations made him remiss in the execution of the ordinary duties of administration.

For a Cistercian abbot these were distinctly onerous, especially if he had daughter-houses to visitate annually, and Rievaulx had five by the time Aelred held office.[29] Presumably for the first ten years of his term, at least until he was granted various indulgences in these matters, Aelred had to face the long journey to the annual general chapter of the Order at Cîteaux, which involved a sea crossing, in addition to the many days he would have to spend on the road. His friend Reginald of Durham has preserved a single anecdote about one of these crossings, which is a reminder of Aelred's fidelity to the popular northern piety in which he had been nurtured. For it seems that he commended the journey to the prayers of St Cuthbert and began to compose some kind of hymn in his honour on the way out to Cîteaux, a fact of which he was only reminded on the way back when, on reaching the coast, he was forced to wait for a fortnight with the English abbots while a prolonged spell of rough weather made it impossible for a boat to set out. The completion of the unfinished hymn brought the awaited opportunity, though this good fortune was confined to the boat that had been placed under Cuthbert's patronage.[30] Even these journeys, which were certainly among the more impersonal and official Aelred was compelled to undertake, probably often also entailed some personal demands upon his time and energy as well as the endurance of their physical fatigues. The only address to a synod of clergy which manuscript tradition locates in a definite city is one Aelred preached at Troyes,[31] presumably on his way through France to or from chapter at Cîteaux. Henry of Carinthia, who was bishop of Troyes throughout the period of Aelred's abbacy, had formerly been a Cistercian monk of Morimond and afterwards an abbot, so that his invitation to a well-known visiting preacher of his own Order perhaps needs no further explanation. From the beginning of his abbacy it was not, however, merely distinguished occasions that determined the routes Aelred took. We first hear of his name as abbot of Rievaulx in connection with the settlement of a dispute about the precedence of the prior of Durham.[32] In that same year, 1147, Savigny, the mother house of a group of reformed monasteries of similar inspiration to those of Cîteaux, submitted to the Cistercian general chapter, and Aelred was soon involved in the affairs of its houses in England. Walter Daniel's father was one of a group of monks sent from Rievaulx to instruct the Savigniac houses of Swineshead in Lincolnshire in Cistercian ways[33] and, when a dispute arose between the abbots of Furness and Savigny about jurisdiction over Byland, Aelred was officially delegated by Cistercian general chapter to give judgement in a matter about which a considerable concourse of English abbots were present to take cognizance.[34] Whether thus in an official capacity, where one nevertheless suspects that his personal reputation as a peace-maker determined his appointment, or in a more private role, Aelred's journeys would often seem to have taken in some such task of arbitration. Walter Daniel relates that some year which is difficult to determine found Aelred visitating Dundrennan and having to work hard for peace in the founding family of Fergus of Galloway.[35] These itineraries naturally had their pleasanter features too. The visitation of Melrose, for instance, also meant a visit to a friend, since Waldef became its abbot in 1148, and Aelred was actually with him in the summer of 1159 when a delegation from St Andrews came in vain to ask Waldef to accept their vacant bishopric.[36] Again Aelred might allow himself a day off to celebrate the feast of St Cuthbert in a little Kirkcudbright church,[37] or call on friends like Reginald at Durham or the hermit Godric out at Finchale, with whom he occasionally even spent the night.[38] But the witnesses which record these facts make it clear that he was still going on with his journeys of visitation long after they were no more imposed upon him as an obligation, and even up to within a matter of months of his death.[39] There is thus independent evidence that Walter Daniel is not blinded by the prejudice of a friend when he insists that, whatever the appearances during attacks of pain and weakness, Aelred as a sick man never became merely soft with himself.

All that government at home and visitations further afield implied it is difficult to assess but, of a man who never appears to have been insensible to a personal tie, it is not possible to believe they can often have failed to demand all and more than he had to give. It is fortunate that we have one minor work, belonging to the earlier period of his abbacy, which may be thought of as illustrative of the way he responded to a claim for spiritual help and guidance, as well as providing us with a gauge of the importance he attached to promoting personal, interior development as the cornerstone of sound government in a healthy monastery. The role of the scriptures in the life of the monk is the frequent burden of Aelred's preaching, and he repeatedly makes it clear that his insistence upon their primacy is due to the fact that they are the gateway to that personal experience of God in every life, which establishes a personal bond that temptation and difficulty cannot break, and which ultimately solves all problems of discipline and asceticism from within. The scriptures are the star that leads us to Jesus,[40] the tomb we must approach like the women on the morning of the resurrection, expectantly carrying our spices of faith, devotion, and love.[41] They are like that field into which we are told, in a verse that Aelred loves to quote, Isaac went out to meditate in the evening.

This field, as it seems to me, is holy scripture, a fertile field indeed, full of every blessing. "Behold," he says, "the smell of my son is as the smell of a plentiful field which the Lord hath blessed." In this field there is the smell of myrrh and incense and every spice of the perfumer. Truly, brethren, there is no virtue, no insight, no wisdom whose smell is not fragrant in this field. And who is full of every blessing, full of every scent of this field, this plentiful field which the Lord hath blessed? Consider. In none of the saints can the fulness of every virtue be found. In David the virtue of humility is specially praised; in Job one detects the smell of patience with a stronger sweetness. Joseph is chaste, Moses is meek, Joshua is strong, Solomon is wise. Yet of none of these can it be said that his smell is like the smell of a plentiful field. In truth the smell of my dearest Lord Jesus is above every perfume, his smell is like the smell of a plentiful field which the Lord hath blessed. Whatever wisdom, whatever virtue, whatever grace is found in the sacred page will all be discovered in him, in whom all the fulness of the godhead dwells corporeally, in whom all the treasures of wisdom and knowledge lie hid, to whom

God does not give the spirit by measure, of whose fulness we have all received.[42]

It is on account of this meeting between the soul and its God that we must come to the scriptures as to the waters of Shiloah "that go with silence".[43]

> This is the teaching of Jesus which is found in holy scripture, which that spirit has written that goes with such silence that "you know not whence he comes or whither he goes". Not thus, not thus the rivers of Egypt, the rivers of Assyria that go with a rush in the wisdom of words that make void the cross of Christ. All *that* learning consists in bandying with words and empty eloquence, blinding rather than enlightening minds with the sophisms of different schools of thought. Your teaching, my good Jesus, is not like that; your waters go with silence. For your teaching, Lord, does not fill the ear with fine-sounding words, but is breathed into the mind by your gentle spirit. Of you it is written: "He shall not contend nor cry out; neither shall any man hear his voice in the streets." So it is heard interiorly, heard in the heart, heard with silence.[44]

The tenor of passages like these is inescapable. They at once evoke an experience and invite the listener to share in it. But the uninitiated may hesitate as to how to begin. It is in a brief work like his *Exposition of the Gospel reading: When Jesus was twelve years old*[45] that Aelred displays how skilfully he could engage the imagination of the beginner and guide him in his first steps in the life of prayer. For, although professedly an exposition of the verses from St Luke's gospel which describe the visit of the boy Jesus to the temple, according to their historical, allegorical, and moral meaning, it is, as its prologue plainly declares, primarily concerned with the development of the life of devotion. Walter Daniel's chronology[46] suggests that this little book was written sometime before 1154. It is addressed to Ivo, a monk of the daughter-house of Wardon, a young friend who reappears in the opening conversation of the later dialogue *On spiritual friendship*, but we may be sure that it admits us to the atmosphere of Aelred's more intimate instructions to any of those who appealed for his spiritual help. For a moment, as he begins, Aelred remembers wistfully the days before he was troubled by the burdens of office.

> Your messenger was telling me of your request and I was feeling in my heart what strong and loving affection had prompted it, when I

suddenly recalled where I once was, what I once felt, what effect those words of the gospel often produced in me when they were being said or sung. Unhappy man, I looked back. I looked back and saw how far behind I had left those pleasant feelings of joy, how far from those delights the bondage of business and of cares had drawn me, so that what my soul would then have disdained to touch, is now in my anguish my daily bread (i, 1).

Then, as he warms to his task, Aelred explains how Jesus goes before us as leader, physician, and teacher along the road we too must tread, foreshadowing in his growth from youth to manhood the stages of our own spiritual development, through formative alternations of darkness and light. "For just as the Lord Jesus is born and conceived in us, so he certainly grows and is nourished in us until we all attain to perfect manhood, to the measure of the stature of the fulness of Christ" (i, 4). Somewhere in the remote background of all this there would seem to be a reminiscence of the ascetic doctrine of Origen with its warm devotion to the person of Jesus. The conversion with which an earnest spiritual life begins is also explained by allusion to the Platonic notion of a return, like that of the prodigal son, from " a land of unlikeness", which is in common use by the early Cistercian writers.[47] Here, as elsewhere, it is easier to believe that Aelred shares their spirit through their common formation and their common sources, rather than through a specific influence from Bernard, by comparison with whom, as far as his teaching on meditative prayer is concerned, he shows himself to be a fresh and original master.

In his exposition of the historical sense Aelred is brief since "you, my son, are not looking for problems, but for devotion" (i, 11). Yet already here he writes graphically in a way which creates a feeling of intimacy with the scenes depicted. "Where were you those three days, good Jesus? Who set food and drink before you? Who made your bed? Who took your shoes off?" (i, 6). This is the secret he will develop into a teachable system. The approach to devotion is through the tears, whether of contrition or of grateful joy, which are the fruit of what Gregory the Great and older monastic writers would have called "compunction".[48] The way in which the soul is stirred to this may be seen by analysing the exquisitely constructed meditation on Mary Magdalen at the feet of Christ, which comes in the third part of his treatise, where Aelred can let his primary concerns come to the fore. There, as he reviews a number of subjects that might be what he has called in his prologue "seeds of holy love" he pauses and makes his monk linger before the house of Simon the Pharisee, whose supper-party was interrupted by the dramatic gesture of the sinful woman with her flask of ointment. "Go into the house", he says, as though leading the beholder through the doorway. "Look closely", he tells him, at the penitent in tears at the feet of Christ, who gazes so kindly upon her. Then, as the imagination becomes captivated by the resonances of the words which recall the woman's kisses, the scent of the ointment and the sight of the beloved feet, one enters into the feelings of the sinner, as one urges her on. "Kiss those feet, O happy sinner, kiss them, clasp them, hold them." Now the contact is made, the attention is held. The sweet odour of the sinner's contrition is contrasted with the smell of death about the Pharisee who despises her. She is "a happy sinner" in having found her own salvation, but "the happiest of all" in having shown the world the place at the feet of Jesus where the leopard may change his spots. This moving reflection is then translated into a reaction involving the one who contemplates the scene too. "What are you doing, O my soul, O my wretched, O my sinful soul? Why do you hold back? Break forth sweet tears, break forth, let nothing impede your course." The monk will weep there until he hears the Lord say to him what he said to the Magdalen in the depths of his soul (iii, 26, 27). That such a response from the Lord should in fact be the soul's experience is only to be expected after long and patient waiting. "Alas, alas, rare the moments and brief the stay", Aelred has said of these experiences, quoting for once a memorable phrase of Bernard.[49] But in this and a later work addressed to his anchoress sister, where he applies his method of meditation to scenes from the entire life of Christ, he shows himself the independent master of a technique which perhaps no one before had grasped so boldly or taught so vividly and clearly. It may be concluded that it was one of the triumphs of his pastoral method that he was able to communicate to others a sense of the possibilities of the life of prayer and of affective contact with the person of Jesus. Certainly it would seem that in those Yorkshire valleys and in the other centres of Cistercian life in England a deep piety, centred upon the person and upon what Aelred calls "the sweet abiding memory of the name"[50] of Jesus came to life in those years. Aelred's meditative technique had a great future before it in later medieval methods of prayer.[51] There his contribution was eventually lost in a mainstream, as perhaps too was his responsibility for a feature of it more distinctive of his own day. For everything points to the fact that it was in England, and not in France, that the tender verses of the *Dulcis Jesu memoria*, "Jesus the very thought is sweet", were born. The temptation to identify Aelred as their author must perhaps be resisted, though his claim is certainly more plausible than that of Bernard.[52] Nevertheless, somewhere in the world from which they came surely lie the lost and unrecorded hours of pastoral endeavour that could occasionally produce a text like that of the exposition of the boyhood visit of Jesus to the temple.

It is, indeed, with the thought of his pastoral responsibilities that the final paragraphs of Aelred's work conclude.

> Suddenly there comes to mind a reminder of the weak, and we think of this man who is sad and awaits some comfort from a father's care, of another, tempted, who is on the look-out for his father to appear and say some helpful word; of that one, upset by the pricks of anger, who complains about his father because he has nowhere to release the poison by making a clean breast of things; of yet another, defeated by depression, who is running round now here, now there, to find someone to talk to and consult.

And so Aelred turns back to his ever-present, inescapable task.

Of the innumerable sermons by which Aelred must have discharged the more formal commitments of his pastoral office, Walter Daniel mentions a collection of about two hundred texts, "if I mistake not".[53] The figure is perhaps a conservative one on any reasonable estimation. But, apart from a late series of homilies on Isaiah, we do not know if Aelred himself prepared any of these sermons for publication. One English manuscript gives what looks like a number of texts which must represent something rather close to the directness and succinctness of the spoken word.[54] For the rest, a surviving manuscript which formerly belonged to the abbey of Clairvaux, contains a series of twenty-seven sermons for the seasons and feasts, with a few incomplete fragments, all the continental libraries can produce today.[55] English manuscripts again preserve an independent collection of something over twenty which were in circulation in homiliaries of contemporary twelfth-century Cistercian preaching. All these latter are edited, not always with great expertise, in the elaborate, often overloaded, literary style in favour for such compositions at the time. Yet even through these, the expressions of an authentic voice can be heard, as the familiar themes from scripture and liturgy are drawn upon to insist that doctrine must be translated into life, so that both the monastery and the heart may become living temples. The touchstone of truth in the things of the spirit is always the common life with our fellow men.

"Receive one another, as Christ also hath received you." You may judge how well Lot teaches us to use hospitality one towards another without murmuring when he who was without the law, or as though without the law, so spontaneously fulfilled the precepts of the law that he received angels as guests. With how much gentleness in the fear of the Lord and with what warmth of charity should we go out to meet our guests, when we have the law written not only in books, but should have it written in our hearts.[56]

A community that realizes this is a community over which the holy spirit broods. In a remarkable Pentecost sermon Aelred once gives us a glimpse of all these notions coordinated. "Today, dearest brethren, I would rather have heard someone else speak than speak myself, would rather hear, indeed, someone who could speak from experience, dipping his pen, as someone has said, in the blood of his heart."[57] He goes on to speak of the image of God in the soul, which is somehow the foundation upon which the possibility of experience is grounded. The soul develops through the secret workings of the Spirit until at last it comes to the true rest of contemplation. This is the fruit of charity, the sweet yoke and the light burden. In truth when anyone gets into that sublime upper room of charity he comes, as it were, to a year of jubilee, fear falls away, labour is turned to rest, sorrow to joy. "Here we are truly made Christ's disciples dwelling *in the same place.* For where there is division there is discord, where there are quarrels and disputes, unbridled desires, ambitions, there indeed there cannot be in the heart identity of place." The spirit is given at Jordan, but with the contrition of the newly converted; on the mountain, but only as passing refreshment in the midst of temptations. "In the upper room, however, *in the same place*, the very fullness of the Spirit is conceived. He was not given before, because Jesus was not yet glorified." This is the point where the life of the monastery passes beyond what can be discussed and enters into a world under the immediate direction of the Spirit.

4

Knights and Kings

These seven orbs turn with a sweet-sounding harmony, and delightful chords are produced by their revolutions. If their sound does not reach our ears, this is because it is made beyond the air and its volume is too great for our limited hearing. For no sound is detected by us unless it is produced in the air. But the music after whose pattern ours is declared to be devised, is measured from earth to the heavenly firmament.[1]

As the libraries of the new English Cistercian abbeys began to grow, they gathered up not merely the source-texts of Christian theology and spiritual doctrine, but a host of diverse information gleaned from the heritage of the past, like this account of the music of the spheres, which ultimately depends upon Pliny's *Natural History*. The passage occurs in one of two important manuscripts from the abbey of Sawley, a house of the family of Fountains, founded on the banks of the Ribble from Newminster in 1148.[2] Competent judges are agreed that these rapidly multiplying houses possessed at first only a small nucleus of books,[3] and that there was often an interval of twenty to thirty years before their *scriptoria* became really productive. Palaeographical indications[4] that most of the surviving new books of these houses are unlikely to have been written before 1170 are confirmed by other considerations arising out of their contents in the case of the two Sawley historical miscellanies.

Aesthetically and imaginatively these two books are profoundly instructive to handle and to read. Both aspire to a universal setting, the one with its sketches and outlines of world history from creation to the emperors and popes of the first quarter of the twelfth century,[5] the other with its map of the world on which the islands of Britain and Ireland are shown in the bottom left-hand corner and Paradise far away at the top, beyond Paris, Rome and the tall, square tower of Babel. A further page delineates Europe and Africa and marks in the old French names of the four winds. Behind the odd mixture of sacred and profane information, fact and fiction, which these pages provide, there is a sense of a world order, half scriptural in basis, half dependent upon the philosophical views of late classical antiquity, such as Pliny's notion of the heavenly exemplars of earthly music calls to mind. A fascination with the remote past is satisfied with the answers to such questions as, "Who was the first king in the world?" or, nearer home, with the works of Gildas and Nennius, which tell of the last days of Roman Britain and the coming of the Saxons. No one could unravel all the sources or assess the value of many of the more unusual facts the often undiscriminating pages of these two books report, but one of them, now Corpus Christi College, Cambridge, MS 139, contains unique copies of several historical writings put together in Northumbria at dates not so remote from the compilation of the manuscript itself, and witnessing to the continuity of a tradition of which Bede had been the chief glory. The most important of these works is a history which consciously looks back to Bede and attempts to carry his work further forward. The Sawley manuscript, in an elaborate title, attributes it to Simeon of Durham, though there are some reasons for supposing that he was the author of only part of it, and that he had perhaps died not long after completing the section which ends in 1129.[6] The *History of the Kings*, as it has come conveniently to be known, often incorporates the work of other writers, but about both Northumbrian affairs, and even about continental history from the days when Northumbrian missionaries were still working with such conspicuous zeal abroad, it appears to draw on primary sources of information which inspire confidence. Two other works unique to this manuscript are attributed to Hexham writers, one dealing with the reign of Stephen and the Battle of the Standard by Richard, a canon of Hexham, and another by John, one of its priors, who continues Simeon's history. The group of documents which relate the beginnings of Fountains, and include Thurstan's letter describing the scenes which led to the departure from St Mary's, York, are, indeed, also to be found elsewhere, but there is no other copy of a letter of Aelred about the case of a nun of the Gilbertine monastery of Watton, just north of Beverley, on which he had been consulted.[7] Again, without the text of Aelred's account of the Battle of the Standard, which this manuscript includes among its pieces devoted to that event, we should not know how that work had ended.[8] The manuscript thus assumes a special importance for the text of two of Aelred's minor historical pieces, but a still greater interest for our understanding of the native milieu under whose influence he devoted so much time in his mature years to writing of a kind for which there is no true parallel among his great Cistercian contemporaries of the founding generation. This manuscript, and its fellow from Sawley, which includes copies of Simeon's history of the Church of Durham, and Richard of Hexham's history of the church of Aelred's birthplace, is a reminder of the strength of the local ties felt in the Yorkshire monasteries of an Order European in its extent and appeal. No portrait of Aelred which failed to take into account his interest in history and its bearing upon the developments of his own day could ever do justice to his many-sided personality. For it is not possible to dismiss as a mere lapse works on which he was engaged with such evidently personal concern while at the very peak of his administrative activity. The Sawley historical manuscripts show how alive these interests were in the world in which he moved and, although there are no signs that Aelred himself ever read more than a few lines of the great Anglo-Norman historian William of Malmesbury, someone at Rievaulx had worked over him with care, as one of the few surviving Rievaulx manuscripts, roughly contemporary with the Sawley histories, reveals.[9] Aelred's less exalted affinities as a historian are more easily defined in terms of the antiquarian mentality of the compilers of the Sawley miscellanies, and of the literary and imaginative character of his own description of the Battle of the Standard.

It is necessary to recall that Aelred's early years as a monk coincided with a period of political anarchy in England. When Henry I died at the beginning of December 1135 "justice and peace, which had long reigned with him in Normandy and England, died too",[10] says Richard of Hexham, using the language of all contemporary observers, who watched the castles of the magnates of the land suddenly spring into terrible importance in the debate about the succession. Henry's only legitimate son, William, had been drowned at sea in 1120, in a splendid ship on board which crew and passengers were alike all drunk, and in the direct line only Henry's unpleasant and unpopular daughter Matilda survived, empress by her first marriage in Germany to Henry V, who had died in 1125, and now by her second marriage wife of Geoffrey of Anjou. Satisfactory Norman alternatives to this pro-Angevin countess were Henry's nephews, the sons of his sister Adela, and the younger of these, Stephen of Blois, a man whose thoroughly likeable qualities even his severest critics admit, was promptly in England as soon as Henry's death was known. Crowned in London before Christmas, his election by such impressive popular support was confirmed by pope Innocent II in the spring of the following year, a fact which Stephen is careful to mention, as giving the highest ecclesiastical sanction to his claim, in his charter of liberties of the same spring, 1136. Yet he was going to have to pay for his authority somewhat dearly. In the north, king David of Scotland, the uncle of the empress Matilda, found that the ostensible support of her cause suited his designs on Northumberland. Hardly was Stephen crowned when David descended with an army, capturing all the border castles with the exception of Bamborough. At the beginning of Lent Stephen advanced to Durham with a show of force sufficient to deter David from pursuing his enterprise for the moment. A peace was agreed, whereby David returned the captured castles, except Carlisle, while his son, Henry, did homage to Stephen at York in return for the honour of Huntingdon, Carlisle, and Doncaster. At Stephen's Easter court in London Henry was even given the place of honour, but it seems that those, including the Archbishop of Canterbury, who thought that Stephen had been too affable and bought the settlement too dearly, conducted themselves in a way which did not conceal their feelings. Their behaviour gave David the pretext to withdraw his son[11] and renew threats which he would doubtless have been able to carry out during Stephen's absence in Normandy but for a strong force at Newcastle, ready to resist him. On Stephen's return, David demanded for his son the earldom of Northumberland, which it was said by some had been promised him at the settlement at York. Stephen, however, was firm and in January 1138 David and Henry moved south again. The atrocities their armies committed are described in vivid and horrible detail by Richard of Hexham, who had good reason to be well-informed about what had happened. Aelred, who of all men had personal motives for wishing to take the most favourable view of his former royal patron, is unable to report differently when he comes to describe the battle which in August was the culmination of the campaign.

There are several contemporary descriptions of the Battle of the Standard, and that Aelred wrote one too is not mentioned by Walter Daniel, though it is listed in the Rievaulx library catalogue,[12] and the volume referred to still survives, though unfortunately the work came near the end of a book whose last leaves are now missing, and consequently it finishes in the middle of a sentence. This and the manuscript from Sawley are our only two early copies[13] of a work that has several marks of having been written for a purpose which it is hard satisfactorily to recover. In the first place, the Rievaulx copy starts with a sentence which suggests not the beginning of a work, but the continuation of something larger. "And so when king Stephen was occupied in the south..." The scribe of the Sawley manuscript has left a sign that he too had this inconsequential beginning before him, for he has prepared the capital letter for its first word,[14] before providing the sentence with a different opening which obscures the suggestion that the entire phrase ought to follow on something which has gone before. It could perhaps be a mere coincidence that an almost identical phrase is in fact the continuation of the narrative in one of the most popular English histories of the period at the point where it reaches the Battle of the Standard,[15] were it not that closer inspection reveals an unmistakable literary relationship between the two accounts at other points too. Henry of Huntingdon's *History of the English* was carried in its first edition as far as 1129, but successive editions eventually brought it down to 1154. Modern historians have never shown any enthusiasm for it, since it is only in appearance a history, being in fact a series of annals mainly based on the Anglo-Saxon Chronicle, lacking in original sources, and never hesitating before any occasion to tell a well-embellished tale. But these were evidently the very qualities that commended it to its welcoming, contemporary public. Aelred's *Battle of the Standard* suggests just the kind of public it was.

Each of the many accounts of the battle has a rather different approach to the facts, but even Henry of Huntingdon, in common with Richard of Hexham and the old life of Archbishop Thurstan of York,[16] makes it clear that it was the archbishop, at least through his representatives, who was the nerve of the opposition to what

Richard of Hexham calls David's "detestable army, more barbarous than any pagans, without reverence for God or man".[17] Old
and sick though he was, it was Archbishop Thurstan who preached
a holy war of defence against the invader. But in Aelred's account,
although this background is also implied, it is really Walter Espec
who is the spokesman for the resistance. During the course of a
long speech before the battle begins Walter, whose age, sagacious
appearance, and enormous voice are emphasized, says:

> It will not be a waste of time for you young heroes to listen to an old
> man who, through the chances of time, the changes of kings, and
> the variable issues of war, has learned to reflect on the past, weigh
> up the present, and surmise about the present from the past, the
> future from the present. I grant you that if all you who are listening
> to me only knew and understood, and foresaw all that would happen
> to us today, I should prefer to hold my peace and lie down for my
> usual sleep, or play at dice or battle with the chessmen or, if those
> seem unsuitable pastimes for a man of my age, then I would occupy
> myself with histories or, as I often do, lend my ear to a teller of the
> deeds of our ancestors.[18]

Had Walter made any such speech before the battle, it is perfectly
credible that he should have confessed to a passion for the battles of
knights, bishops, and kings on the chessboard, since this seems to
have been common at the period. Of his connection with the circle
of those who liked reading histories we have independent evidence
from the fact that it was through his good offices that Lady
Fitzgilbert, the patroness of the Anglo-Norman poet Gaimar, was
able to obtain from Duke Robert of Gloucester a copy of Geoffrey
of Monmouth's history which told of the doings of king Arthur.[19]
According to Aelred, Walter had that gift of fair speech which we
should expect to go with the interests of the lay patrons of such
writings.[20] He liked to listen to a well-told story. Was it, then, he
who insisted, as one who had played his part in it, that Henry of
Huntingdon's account of the battle of the Standard did not do
justice to the facts, and that someone ought to write another account
of what had really happened? There is, at any rate, a Rievaulx
tradition that Walter Espec was still alive at a date which would
make such a suggestion possible.[21]

For Aelred's *Battle of the Standard* is certainly warfare recollected
in tranquillity, and although Northallerton, where the battle was
fought, is not so far from Rievaulx on the map, Aelred's writing

could scarcely be further than it is from the physical realities of the battlefield. We shall look in vain in his description for tellingly reported observations of fact like, for instance, the rising of the morning mist mentioned in the continuation of the chronicle of Florence of Worcester,[22] and even one of Aelred's most frequently cited phrases, which describes David's Galwegian soldiers as stuck all over with arrows like hedgehogs, certainly has a literary source which Aelred knew. Talking one day to Reginald of Durham about his own ancestry, Aelred seems to have alluded to it in its original context, as it was used by Abbo of Fleury in his description of the passion of St Edmund, the king and martyr.[23] It is, again, to Richard of Hexham that we must go if we wish to know what the Standard, after which the battle was called, actually was. For it seems to have been a pole as big as a ship's mast, surmounted by a silver pyx containing the Reserved Sacrament, below which the banners of the local patrons of the fight, St Peter the Apostle to represent York, St John of Beverley, and St Wilfrid of Ripon, moved in the wind. Richard quotes some lines from a lost poem by an archdeacon of York, which connect the name of the battle with the English word "to stand",[24] though in fact it is derived from the French word *estandard*. Now here we touch on an area of possible confusions and a level of contemporary reality on which Aelred really was something of an expert and around which he builds his narrative with careful artistry.

His interests are in fact in people and ideas and, if he does not actually report their very words, we may be confident that he makes them say what they would have wished to have said. In this way he has a great deal to tell us. Although, like Henry of Huntingdon, Aelred names the young William of Albemarle first among the leaders on the field, the real hero of his piece is Walter Espec with his black hair, drawn features, long beard, and large, penetrating eyes. He is in the centre of the picture as it were by double right. The domestic piety of a monk of Rievaulx is unwilling to miss so favourable an occasion for depicting the virtues of the founder, "noble by birth, but nobler still in his Christian goodness." Aelred thus digresses upon Walter's various religious foundations, upon the circumstances which brought the Cistercians to England and gave Rievaulx so special a place in the propagation of their way of life, Walter Espec himself providing for the first of its daughter houses. But Walter also serves as the mouthpiece for the sentiments that are expressed in Huntingdon's account by Ralph, Bishop of the Orkneys.[25] In either case, we are reminded that the "English" defenders against David's invasion are all of them conscious first and foremost of being Normans and when, in a speech which follows the pattern of "circumstances" laid down in the classical textbooks of rhetoric, Walter asks the army who they are, why they are there, and what they are fighting for, it is not to a local past, recalled by the banners at the masthead, that he appeals.

Why should we despair of victory, when victory has been given to our race by the Most High, as though it were our due? [he asks]. Did not our grandfathers invade the greater part of Gaul with a handful of soldiers and wipe out with the people even the name? It is a fact that this island, which once the victorious Julius, not without heavy losses and after many years, scarcely at length secured, we speedily subdued, rapidly subjected to our laws and bound to our allegiance. We saw, yes, we saw with our very eyes the king of France with his whole army turn their backs on us, the noblest flower of his kingdom taken by us, some to be ransomed, some to be bound in chains, some condemned to prison. Who tamed Apulia, Sicily, Calabria, if it was not your Norman?[26]

It is enough to read the names of the leaders of the defending army and the details of their support to appreciate how exactly Aelred's rhetorical invention reflects the true state of affairs in what he as easily refers to as the "southern" as to the "English" army. William of Albemarle and Walter de Gant[27] are there with a company of Flemish and Norman knights. The grandfather of Ilbert de Laci had been given Pontefract and Blackburnshire by the Conqueror, and Robert de Brus was also the son of a Norman who had acquired many manors in Yorkshire. As a friend of king David, probably from the days when they were together at the court of Henry I, Aelred has a special interest in him.[28] Roger de Mowbray owned estates which were divided only by the river Rye from those of Walter Espec. Walter's speech refers explicitly to the cause of king Stephen, to his election, and the confirmation of his authority by the pope. "But", Walter continues, evidently with his eye on this Yorkshire group of Norman landlords, "to say nothing of the king for the moment, certainly no just man will deny that we have taken up arms *pro patria*; that we are fighting for our wives, our children, our churches, repelling an imminent peril." It is through these lands, these homes, and these churches that England has become their own country.

But the situation was more painfully complex still. Of the two sons of Robert de Brus, Aelred tells us that Adam, who eventually succeeded to the English estates, was with his father. He does not mention that the other son, Robert, heir to the Scots estates in Annandale,[29] was fighting for king David. Aelred does, however, contrive to make it clear that one of the tragedies of this war was that it was a war between friends. No other writer knew the leaders on both sides better than he, and when he gives us a picture of what went on in the opposing camps, he underlines how much they had in common. For when we pass over to king David's camp, we find him having to argue with his Galloway men, because he wishes to place his well-armed and mounted English and Norman forces in the front line. Unmoved by arguments of a previous success at Clitheroe, he has to yield when Malise, Earl of Strathearn, at last breaks in and asks angrily why the king so openly favours his foreign "frenchmen". And so the contending armies are drawn up, the southern army in a solid phalanx with archers spaced between the lances. Walter Espec, who presumably refers contemptuously to the kilt when he speaks of the Scots as preceded by "actors, dancers, and dancing-girls", but who also has his atrocity stories of the Galloway men, now sees them in the front line. Prince Henry and the Cumbrians are in the second line, the men of the isles in the third, the Moray men and David's Norman bodyguard in the fourth.

There is then a last-minute attempt at a parley on the part of Robert de Brus. His speech, a tribute to a man whom Aelred evidently knew and admired, is also an important contribution to our knowledge of the significance of Norman support for king David. During the course of what he has to say, he reveals that just as it was Norman intervention that put David on the throne at all so, as far back as the crisis after the death of king Malcolm, it was only the threat of Norman force which had secured David his rights against his brother Alexander. Robert gives full vent to his emotions as he reminds David of their friendship from youth, of their hunts and military exercises and of the splendid banquets they sat down to, when they were together. His tears flow as he points out that the Scots, whom David finds it so difficult to handle, will be the only ones to be pleased by a breach between them now.

David, like Robert and other knights of the period, is not ashamed now to be weeping too and is almost won over, but for a final reminder of the inexorable realities of his situation. William Fitzduncan the, probably illegitimate, son of king Duncan II, and a man whom Aelred says was the principal instigator of the campaign, bursts into an uncontrollable rage at what he regards as a betrayal. David evidently could not afford to displease a possible rival for his throne, and so with a heavy heart Robert de Brus renounces his enfeoffment to David and returns to the southern lines.

When the battle was joined what David had foreseen was justified by the event. The Galwegians with their primitive equipment were no match for the Norman defenders and those who were not killed were soon scattered in flight. According to one report, David himself narrowly escaped, reaching Roxburgh through the wild woods, while his son, Henry, came to Carlisle on foot in the company of a single soldier.[30] Of his gallant attempt to save the situation in the field, when the king's banner turned in the rout, Aelred has a concluding word of praise.[31] It enables him to put the last touches to the portrait of a friend he had loved from his boyhood. In describing the Scots forces, he has already spoken of Henry's physical beauty and his winning combination of human and religious virtues, singling out his prowess for special mention.[32] Now, "calm in difficulty", we see him spurring his horse into the ranks of the defenders in order to make a cover for the retreat. Only at last, when his armour has become a burden rather than a help, does he give his heavy corselet to a poor cottager in a final gesture of generous compassion. Henry is thus the complete exemplar of romantic chivalry.

Back in Carlisle, father and son met to recover their shattered forces. But not until April 1139 did intermediaries have the satisfaction of seeing the signing of peace. King Stephen's position was by that time serious enough to persuade him to grant Henry the earldom of Northumberland, which the king had earlier refused. In England the trouble continued for many years yet, but after this David devoted his chief energies to his work for Scotland, and of his achievements in that direction Aelred has left us a sympathetic and informative estimate in a more extended piece of writing, linked to a treatise consciously designed to promote the interests of peace.

It is very difficult to determine at what date Aelred wrote his description of the Battle of the Standard, but, if the internal signs of its relationship to Henry of Huntingdon's *History of the English* have been correctly envisaged, it cannot have been before the close of 1154, when the latest edition of Huntingdon's work was completed, just after the arrival of the young Henry II in England. 1155 is thus the earliest probable date[33] and by that time King David of Scotland had already long been dead. Besides the personal grief he felt, David's death on 24 May 1153 must have filled Aelred with anxiety for the future of all that had been accomplished in Scotland during the latter years of his reign for, only a few months before, the premature death of Earl Henry on 12 June 1152 had left David with a grandson of eleven as his heir. As he sat down to embody his double grief in one of the great laments of the period, Aelred did not perhaps see at first how best to be helpful at a moment when it seemed possible that the anarchy in England might also spread to Scotland. Only gradually did the idea of the work he finally published evolve in his mind, and then it retained the marks of its hesitant origin.

As Walter Daniel tells us, Aelred began with a life of David in the form of a lament.[34] It is really a funeral oration with the memory of the old Greek and Latin oratorical forms behind it. Thus it opens with an introduction followed by a summary of the virtues of its subject and a lament for his loss. This is developed through a series of themes illustrating his moral qualities and achievements, and the discourse is rounded off by an exhortation and prayer. In this form the fourth-century Fathers Gregory Nazianzen and Gregory of Nyssa in the East and Ambrose in the West had adopted and christianized the tradition they had inherited from their literary education. Among his Cistercian contemporaries Aelred had a moving and eloquent example in the lament for his brother Gerard with which Bernard had concluded his twenty-sixth sermon on the *Song of Songs*, and he had himself written a similar lament for his friend Simon, while he was putting together his *Mirror of Charity*.[35] The intimacy of either of these would have been inappropriate to this more formal occasion and in his lament for David Aelred strives after a more grandiloquent effect. "The religious and devout king David has departed this life and, although he has found a place worthy of such a soul, his death requires of us a lament. For who would not mourn a man so necessary to the world?"[36] As the allusions to scripture begin to accumulate they are skilfully chosen to establish the solemn tempo the writer desires to achieve. Aelred naturally has in mind the biblical laments of David for Saul and Jonathan and of Jeremiah for the fallen and deserted Jerusalem, but his summary of David of Scotland's virtues is chiefly expressed in the language of the book of *Ecclesiasticus* when it praises the memory of Moses "beloved of God and men". The virtues Aelred singles out for special comment are humility, justice, and chastity. David endeared himself to everyone by a combination of virtues un-common in a king, who being the source of power may be thought to be allowed to do what he pleases,[37] and whose example is correspondingly more important for his people. David illustrates the dictum of scripture that "it is the meek who inherit the earth", in so far as, although he was free of the desire to dominate, his humility enabled him to control the land of his inheritance, unlike his ancestors before him. He was dear to God, too, for his foundation and support of churches and monasteries. Later in the lament Aelred mentions a visit to David in connection with the needs of his own house, which occurred during the last Lent of the king's life.[38] Thus the cause for tears at David's death is shared by all classes of society. The king is depicted as endlessly patient with and concerned for the administration of justice to the poor and oppres-sed, while on the other hand his social influence extends to every aspect of national living "to gardens, buildings, and orchards". All this in praise. Yet it has also to be admitted that, like his namesake in scripture, David did sin greatly, though it was not against chastity, where his name is unsullied. For when every excuse has been made in the name of oaths and promises, it still remains true that the king should never have led his savage and undisciplined army against the English in the way that he did on more than one occasion. Even here, however, there is matter for consolation. David did repent, and only the needs of his kingdom prevented him from taking the Crusader's Cross. He was, moreover, purged by provi-dential trials both public and personal, which he bore with patience as justly sent by God. His dispositions during the last year of his life could not have been more exemplary, and he died as though he were going to sleep. Aelred concludes his lament with a fine prayer based on a liturgical text from the burial rites, which asks the saints and angels to come and fetch the departed soul, and he declares that he will always remember the king at the sacrifice of the Mass, "where the Son is daily offered to the Father for the salvation of all".

It is neither necessary nor profitable to analyse the mass of allusions to the bible in which Aelred's lament for David abounds. They are part of its very texture, and would come naturally enough to a man accustomed to their frequent use in the liturgy. Indeed, even today, for a man used to the regular celebration of the Latin liturgy they would mostly be commonplaces. The same may be said of the frequent reminiscences of the Rule of St Benedict, in a writer living under and officially commissioned to interpret that Rule. In particular, the portrait of the ideal abbot in chapter two of the Rule would evidently often be appropriate to the portrait of a king administering in a somewhat patriarchal manner a still primitive society. None of this language detracts from the seriousness of Aelred's purpose or the genuineness of his estimate of David's life and character. These are almost guaranteed by Aelred's willingness to admit that no defence can be made for David's bellicose expeditions into England. Indeed, when Aelred's conventions, assertions, and hints are correctly interpreted, they give us an invaluable impression of David's aims and achievements in a reign that had lasted almost thirty years.

At his accession in 1124 David, brought up in religious ways by a mother with a reputation for holiness, and used to the manners of a Norman court, found himself, as Aelred says, "among a barbarous people, hostile to each other on account of differences of language and custom, deadly enemies by reason of mutual deaths and injuries". How mixed they were, and what difficulties it led to, is suggested with sufficient vividness at the battle of the Standard. Not only did David find in Scotland an agglomeration of peoples which were scarcely a nation, he found a Church administered by no more than three or four bishops, a clergy relaxed and deficient in numbers, and a land in which the religious life of the monasteries was almost unknown. Gardening and agriculture were little practised, trade was undeveloped, and the towns, where they existed, were in every way backward. All this, Aelred argues, David changed, and he did it by his personal energy and initiative. He is pictured as taking an interest in everything and talking to everyone, so that his administration and his justice gradually spread their controls everywhere. To achieve this, he never spared himself and

Aelred mentions having himself seen the king, about to leave for a day's hunting, turn aside at the request of a poor man for justice.

> Sitting at the door of the royal hall, he was accustomed to hear the cases of the poor and the widows who were summoned on certain days from the district he happened to have reached, and he would satisfy each, often at great pains. For they would frequently argue with him and he with them, since he was unwilling to favour the person of the poor contrary to justice, and they were unwilling to acquiesce in the arguments he put forward.[39]

If this description strikes a primitive note, and reminds one of the manner in which a chieftain might administer justice to his clan, David's purposes were more sophisticated. Under his influence the clothes people wore and the houses they lived in were different. The ports grew busy with the trade their needs encouraged.

> He adorned you with castles and cities. He raised your high towers. He filled your ports with foreign merchandise, and gathered for your delights the riches of other nations. He changed your homespun for fine clothing, and covered your wonted nakedness with linen and purple. He tamed your wild manners with the Christian religion.[40]

David brought about his religious changes by increasing his bishoprics and furthering the ecclesiastical organization that went with them, while he founded or protected monasteries of every important type of continental observance. Aelred gives a list, most of which can confidently be identified. There were Cluniacs of David's own foundation on the Isle of May at the mouth of the Firth of Forth. His Cistercian house of Melrose, a colony from Rievaulx, had three daughter foundations before the end of his reign, that of Holm Cultram being under the patronage of his son Henry. Either Fergus of Galloway or David himself brought another Rievaulx colony to Dundrennan in 1142. The Tironese monks, whom David had brought to Selkirk while he was still an earl, were moved to Kelso soon after his accession, and one of the greatest of his subjects, Hugh de Moreville, founded two other houses for them which, like David, he filled with monks direct from France. The canons of Arrouaise in Picardy came to Cambuskenneth in 1147, and the Premonstratensians to Dryburgh in 1150. It is probable that Aelred also refers to the canons of St Quentin-les-Beauvais at Jedburgh Priory. In addition the Templars are mentioned, and some unspecified nuns who may be the Cistercian sisters at South Berwick.[41]

7

All these social and religious innovations were not brought about without difficulty and considerable opposition, over which Aelred prefers to draw the veil of silence. Aelred pictures David unperturbed in the last months of his life, leading a half monastic life in a court that was like a cloister, with its observance of the canonical hours and even, to warm the heart of a Cistercian, a little time set aside for manual labour in the garden. David dies as he venerates the cross of his mother Queen Margaret. Finely worked in gold and filigree, this remarkable object is described in detail by Aelred, who makes it clear that it must have been a splendid piece of *opus Anglicanum*,[42] fittingly symbolic of David's religious and civilizing aspirations.

No other contemporary historian has so much to say of David, but what they do say confirms the impression Aelred seeks to convey. To Henry of Huntingdon he is "the urbane king".[43] To John of Hexham "there was no prince like him in our days. It was praiseworthy in him that in the spirit of counsel and fortitude he wisely controlled the savagery of his barbarous people.[44] William of Malmesbury believed that his education in England has made him "more of a courtier" than his brothers. "When he finally succeeded to the throne, he at once remitted three years taxation to all his fellow-countrymen who wished to live in a more civilized way, to dress better and keep a good table".[45] "And so," Orderic Vitalis would add, "David, his power extended, was exalted above his predecessors, and by his zeal the kingdom of Scotland was filled with devout and learned people".[46] Coloured as they are by rhetoric, these appraisals nevertheless give David a consistent reputation as a power for effective change. One scholar who devoted years to weighing the evidence concluded that its tenor could be expressed in three words: David Normanized Scotland.[47] To all that was positive for good in this no one owed more than Aelred, who had benefited from it in his youth. After Earl Henry's untimely death he must have shared to the full the king's concern for the survival of what had been achieved. David was leaving only grandsons to succeed him.

But [says Aelred in his lament] the age of a king is to be measured by the faith of his knights. Pay the sons what you owed the father; let them find you grateful for the benefits you received. Moreover, let the perils of the English teach you to keep faith with kings, to preserve mutual concord among yourselves, lest foreigners devour your land before you, and it be laid waste as in the devastation of war.

It is unfortunate that, so far, no trace of Aelred's extensive correspondence, to which Walter Daniel refers, has been recovered, for it is probable that, among other things, it would throw light on any personal intervention of Aelred to promote peace in England during the reign of Stephen. Walter Daniel specifically mentions the importance of his connection with the Earl of Leicester,[48] whose treaty with Rannulf, Earl of Chester, during the latter years of Stephen, shows two great feudal landlords attempting to deal with the problems of their personal relationships in default of the control of an effective central government.[49] Did Aelred, one wonders, have any part in this move towards the recognition of the need for order? Certainly in 1153 David's death encouraged him to think on the national level and, in his own mind, to link the fate of England and Scotland together. For already by 1145 Geoffrey of Anjou had made himself master of Normandy, where he wisely chose to rule virtually as the regent for his young son Henry who had, through his mother the Empress Matilda, a rightful claim to the duchy. Henry had claimed to be the legitimate heir to the throne of England since he was a boy of ten and his education, which had included a stay at Bristol between 1142–4 with Duke Robert of Gloucester, a patron of learning and letters, had prepared him for a great future. This seemed to be opening before him when, as a boy of sixteen, he had been knighted by David of Scotland in a solemn Pentecost ceremony at Carlisle in 1149.[50] The plot to oust Stephen, hatched at the same feast, came to nothing, but back in Normandy his father the count transferred the duchy entirely to him in 1150. By his marriage with Eleanor, the former queen of King Louis VII of France, he became duke of Aquitaine in May 1152. In the January of 1153 Henry, freed from the wars in France, was ready to return to England to make good his claim. As the months went by, it must have become clear that for the first time Henry was at last leading a successful campaign against Stephen, whose eldest son Eustace died in August. In November the terms of a treaty, whereby the young Henry became Stephen's heir, had been worked out. In the following spring Henry returned to Normandy, but he had not long to wait, for Stephen died on 25 October 1154.

This was the news that had been coming in during the months of 1153 while Aelred was writing his lament for king David, and in the hope that it might find a sympathetic audience for his plea on behalf of David's heirs in Scotland Aelred, to use Walter Daniel's expression, decided to add to it a work addressed and dedicated to the young duke Henry, not yet king.[51] Although, as Walter Daniel says, these were published "in one book", they do not in fact make a literary unity. For the second part is a genealogy of the young Henry's royal ancestry in England, a history whose purpose is to point a moral and adorn a tale. Indeed the imaginative and didactic purpose behind them is the only real link between the two parts. The whole work is evidently meant to be a "mirror for kings", perhaps the earliest twelfth-century example of a type of literature which had Carolingian forbears in treatises of men like Alcuin and Hincmar of Rheims.[52] Aelred's *Genealogy of the Kings* combines its admonitory information with a demonstration of Henry's tenuous claim to blood descent from Edward the Confessor in a way which shows it also to be an attempt at a reasoned reconciliation of the Anglo-Saxon past and the Norman present.

Aelred takes as the starting-point of his narrative the genealogy of king Aethelwulf, which occurs in the Old English Chronicle under the year 855, and was used by his biographer Asser for the family pedigree of Aethelwulf's son, king Alfred. The Saxon kings in England had commonly claimed to be descended from gods, generally from Woden. When they became Christian, Woden was not forgotten, but transformed. The Fathers of the Church had shown the way, in adopting the theory of an early third-century romance by Euhemerus, who had given the gods an historical existence. Augustine and Isidore were two of the channels of its transmission. In effect it gave the gods a new prestige by enabling them to be fitted into a line stretching back to Adam, the father of the human race,[53] and thus Woden appears in Aelred's *Genealogy*. Whether in pagan or in Christian times the royal house was thereby invested with a divine sanction. What this meant imaginatively in the twelfth century may be judged by looking at the splendid page from one of the history books of Sawley abbey where Woden appears, larger than life in his kingly majesty, his face with its enormous, penetrating eyes suggesting both the terror and the wisdom of authority.[54]

Aelred begins his individual sketches of the kings with Aethelwulf, and the fortunes of the Saxon line are traced with more or less detail from Alfred to the troubled reign of king Aethelred. The note of Church reform is struck throughout, and Saxon devotion to the Holy See, which needed no invention, is heavily under-lined. Alfred, we are told, "thought it no part of a king's high dignity to have power in the Church of Christ, a view which one rarely finds in the world today".[55] But the submissiveness to be expected from kings is not inconsistent in Aelred's mind with their having a very real part to play in ecclesiastical reform. With some sense of historical plausibility Aelred puts into the mouth of king Edgar, in a speech addressed to Dunstan, an interesting statement of the doctrine of the two swords. "I hold in my hand the sword of Constantine, you that of Peter," Edgar declares to Dunstan. "Let us join our right arms, let us link sword to sword that the lepers may be cast out of the camp, that the sanctuary of the Lord may be cleansed".[56] These words, and those which precede them, suggest a distinctly moderate view of the relation between the temporal and the spiritual powers. Here Aelred seems to imply that Church and king are joining right arm to right arm as, in some sense, equal representatives of two different kinds of authority, and in a speech which is, after all, a pure invention he is content to represent the king as taking the initiative. On the other hand, when preaching on the royal aspect of their office to the clergy in synod at Troyes on another occasion, he will say: "You are kings, and as much higher than earthly kings as the heavenly kingdom is above the earthly. They rule the bodies of men, you rule their souls. They bear the material sword, to you is committed the spiritual one. They dispense earthly things, you minister the heavenly. It is theirs to give temporal goods to their subjects, yours to grant the eternal".[57] Yet even this passage develops into a discourse on self-control, and is perhaps consistent with a view of kingship more like that of the monastic reformers of Edgar's reign than that of many of Aelred's contemporaries.

If Aelred is able to regard the young duke Henry, to whom the work is addressed, as "the hope of the English", this is because his conciliatory mind sees in him a symbolic union of the Saxon and Norman peoples. To make this view cogent it is necessary to organize the facts from the reign of Aethelred onwards with a certain dexterity. Aelred does not confuse us with details. The short sketch of Aethelred tells us little save of his marriage to the Norman Emma, and of her flight with her two children, Edward and Alfred, during the Danish invasions. Aethelred's successor, Edmund Ironside, a son by a former marriage, is then described in heroic proportions in his struggle with Cnut for the possession of the kingdom, and a tournament, fought on an island in the Severn between the two champions, conveniently symbolizes the long disturbances that preceded the return of Edward the Confessor from Normandy. The dramatic outline of this far-fetched story is found in Henry of Huntingdon,[58] but Aelred takes it up with all the verve of the *raconteur*. "Not my powers alone, but those of a Virgil, nay even of a Homer, would fail before such a theme",[59] he asserts. The two champions put up a glorious show of shivered lances and flashing swords and the incident ends with Edmund Ironside, at heart a gentle man, leaning on his long shield to listen to a speech of king Cnut. Cnut manages this, in spite of being as breathless with admiration for his opponent as he is with the effort of parrying his blows. The two decide upon a pact of brotherhood and exchange the kiss of peace. Edmund Ironside has here been made the type of the contemporary ideal of chivalry. He has an invincible strength of body, but it is not this physical strength that makes him the man he is. It is his happy combination of apparently opposite virtues. Against his enemies he has the fierceness of a lion, but with his friends the simplicity of a dove. He is strong but gentle, bold yet careful. He is reliable, unperturbed in difficulties, modest in success. In fact he has about him the marks of Aelred's friend Earl Henry of Scotland. His prowess is wonderful.

Aelred knew his audience, and this engaging tale provides a romantic interlude in a somewhat meaty argument. The exile of Edmund Ironside's children to Hungary after his death is mentioned to prepare us for their return under the Confessor, Cnut and his successors being disposed of in a single sentence. At this point the future biographer of Edward the Confessor keeps his account of Edward's reign remarkably short, so as to give prominence to the arrival from abroad of Edmund Ironside's only son Edward with his wife, Agatha, and their three children Edgar, Margaret, and Christina. Scarcely has the royal party arrived in London when Edward, the father, dies and soon after him the Confessor too. The young Prince Edgar is set aside on account of his age and, with the help of arms and moneybags, Harold becomes king. At this, William, Duke of Normandy, justly the heir by blood, prepares an army to invade. In the midst of the confusion Prince Edgar decides to return to Hungary with his mother and sisters, but their ship is blown out of course on to the coast of Scotland, a happy providence, because there Margaret meets and marries king Malcolm. Christina becomes a nun, and Margaret bears the king six sons and two daughters. Three of the sons, Edgar, Alexander, and David, become successively kings of Scotland, while of the daughters one marries Henry I and becomes Queen Maud of England and the other, Mary, marries Eustace Count of Boulogne. It is these matches that lead to the relationship between David of Scotland and his nephew Duke Henry, to their common relationship with Edward the Confessor, and their common descent through king Aethelred from Alfred the Great.

The imaginative element in this work that must have been completed only a month or two before the young Henry II became king of England in October 1154 has been emphasized, as its author's purpose intended. "For to know that one is privileged with noble blood from the best families is the strongest incentive to moral effort, since any right-minded man is ashamed to prove himself the degenerate one of a glorious line." Through his stories about the past Aelred expresses his ideals and hopes for the coming reign. As such, even where they are fiction, they are historically valuable to us now. But the *Genealogy of the Kings* is much more than a work of the creative imagination. An analysis of the historical information on which it is built reveals that it presupposes the continuous study of at least one major chronicle. It is not altogether easy to decide which. If it was Simeon of Durham's *History of the Kings*, then it must have been supplemented by other documents on early kings and early royal foundations. Florence of Worcester would have sufficed more completely, save for the story of the gifts which Alfred is said to have received from the patriarch of Jerusalem, known only to the sources of Simeon and Asser's *Life of Alfred*. In Alfred Aelred has a rather special interest and his full and compact section on Alfred's life suggests the use of a number of subsidiary sources. The anecdote of the emperor Constantine's refusal to judge the clergy comes either directly from Rufinus or from the forged decretals,[60] while the account of the appearance of St Cuthbert to Alfred in the marshes comes, most probably, from the Durham document *Concerning the miracles and translations* of that saint.[61] It may be that Aelred is dependent upon a text of the Old English Chronicle for his knowledge of Alfred's capture of the Dane's Raven banner, for it is not mentioned by Asser, Florence, or Simeon, and evidently he has come across a book of Alfred's

parables and laws.[62] From writers nearer his own day he has drawn
the story of Dunstan's rescue of Eadwig's soul from the devils, first
told in Osbern of Canterbury's *Life of Dunstan*,[63] and to Henry of
Huntingdon he owes the basis of his tale of the fight between
Edmund Ironside and king Cnut. From him too may come the
story of Edmund's being murdered in a latrine. He certainly implies
that he is aware of Huntingdon's tradition about the death of
Swein. Finally, not only had king David himself told him the two
stories about king Malcolm and Queen Maud which he recounts,
but Aelred would seem also himself to be the source of the tradition
of king Aethelstan's visit to the shrine of St John of Beverley,[64] and
for the statement that the mother of Edmund Ironside was the
daughter of Thored.[65]

In brief, none of Aelred's writings can have cost him more
thought and care. His critical faculty is not altogether asleep, as we
may see in his report of the two traditions of the death of Swein,
though he might have been expected to be captivated by Florence's
more dramatic account. In any case, he always re-writes and re-
arranges his material with real discrimination. His monastic idealism is naturally always there in the background, as in his amusing
transformation of the somewhat earthbound Durham version of
Alfred's vision of St Cuthbert, where Aelred has eliminated the
king's wife and represents Alfred himself as being rather glad to be
in the marshes at Athelney because they afford better opportunities
for contemplation. Yet modifications of this kind are introduced
with considerable restraint, and perhaps the greatest concession to
the literary taste of the times is the introduction in the narrative of
one long prayer and about five speeches of varying lengths. It was,
perhaps, his ability to marshal the evidence and put it forward in
language his contemporaries found impressive that brought him,
within the next ten years, a commission which he doubtless regarded
as the opportunity to set the seal upon the conciliatory work for
England which he had initiated in his *Genealogy of the Kings*.

When Edward the Confessor died on 5 January 1066 his body was
buried the following day in the great abbey church of St Peter at
Westminster, whose consecration on 28 December of the previous
year he had been too ill to attend. The building had been one of the
chief preoccupations of his closing years, being an architectural
monument to the peaceful penetration of Norman influence before
the Conquest. Wholly Norman in inspiration, it was the first royally

magnificent church of its kind to be seen in England.[66] It was only gradually that the monks of Westminster came to realize that they had a treasure almost equally unique in the body of its founder. Yet, even within a short time after his death, his reputation for holiness and miracles had found expression in a *Life*[67] that does not appear to have been motivated either by the interests of the abbey or of any of the political theories which were later to fasten upon it. Whoever its author may have been, he stands, like his subject, as it were somewhere between the Anglo-Saxon and the Norman worlds, and in what he says we can discern the essentials of the tradition about Edward, before its possibilities have been exploited.[68] Already at the tomb where Edward's body is laid "washed by his country's tears", in furtherance of what had happened even during his life, "the blind receive their sight, the lame the strength to walk, the sick are healed, the sad revived by the comfort of God".[69]

After the Conquest the first official recognition by the abbey authorities of the growth of a limited popular cult of king Edward appears to have been the opening of his tomb in 1102 by one of Anselm's former pupils, Abbot Gilbert Crispin. Another of Anselm's pupils, Gundulph, Bishop of Rochester, was also present when the stone was lifted, and the body was found to be lying there incorrupt, laid out in the royal robes.[70] The awed investigators left it undisturbed, and no further steps were taken until in 1138 the Prior of Westminster, Osbert of Clare, wrote a life of Edward, from which we learn of the recognition of the body thirty-six years previously. This life Osbert submitted to the papal legate, Alberic of Ostia, who was in England towards the end of that year, in the hope that he would canonize Edward.[71] But the legate refused, and seems to have advised that Osbert should take his case to Rome, with evidence of impressive support for his petition. To this end Osbert went to pope Innocent II with a letter from king Stephen and others from various ecclesiastical dignitaries. The pope, however, again refused to comply with Osbert's request, perhaps perceiving something of its personal and domestic character, and asking for evidence that it genuinely represented a national demand. There were possibly many other considerations to suggest the advisibility of delay, but these can only be a matter of conjecture.

After another long lapse of time the documents and, most probably, the life which Innocent II had seen were again inspected by pope Alexander III, who had received a new series of petitions for

Edward's canonization from Henry II and at least eight of the English bishops as well as the abbot and chapter of Westminster.[72] It is clear that Abbot Laurence of Westminster had been very energetic in presenting a well-prepared case, such as Innocent II had earlier required, and Alexander III responded by canonizing Edward in two bulls issued from Anagni on 7 February 1161.[73] One bull was addressed to the Westminster community and the other to the bishops, abbots, and clergy of England. The king's association with the petition is specifically alluded to by the pope, and a number of circumstances, including the apparently unwonted promptness with which the pope acted, have led to the supposition that political pressure was the really operative factor in the decision.[74] It is true that Alexander's election in September 1159 had been followed by the setting up of a pro-imperial anti-pope, and that the support of Henry II of England was important to Alexander. It is also true that at least the petition of Gilbert Foliot, bishop of Hereford, makes open play with the notion that king Henry's adherence to the pope, made public in the autumn of 1160, deserves some suitable recognition of the kind proposed.[75] To which of the parties in the schism England would finally adhere must, indeed, have seemed problematic for many months. A long letter of John of Salisbury on the subject speaks of the efforts of the dying Archbishop Theobald of Canterbury to win over the clergy of England, and of the firmness of the archbishop of York, but indicates that at least the bishops of Winchester and Durham were believed to be hesitant.[76] The news of Alexander's election had been brought to England in 1159 by messengers from a Cistercian abbot, and Aelred, in common with his Order, came out decisively in the pope's support.[77] It is even possible that, like Bishop Arnulf of Lisieux, who devoted himself to intense activities in this direction,[78] Aelred wrote some kind of tract on the subject, which has now been lost.[79] One late chronicle associates Aelred's efforts with those of Arnulf and actually declares that it was Aelred who won the king over *viva voce*.[80] This at least is extremely unlikely, since Henry II was absent from England during the whole period from 1158 to the autumn of 1163, and Aelred had already been given his wide discretionary powers about travel and physical effort. Even if Arnulf of Lisieux' boast that it was he, "first and alone",[81] who had persuaded Henry is not true, Alexander wrote to him, with evident relief, as though he believed it.[82] There is, then, no denying that

Alexander had his reasons for wishing to retain the allegiance of Henry II and the people of England.

Yet, considered as a whole, the letters begging for the canonization, which Alexander received, speak of a reputation for holiness that can be traced back to the immediate circle of the Confessor himself, and then there is the undoubted witness of the incorrupt body, a piece of whose shroud, intact for almost a century, abbot Laurence had sent to two cardinal legates, whose letter was in the dossier.[83] If the mysterious growth of the cult of St Edward was indeed to be turned to the political advantage of Henry II, it had certainly developed under political conditions very different from those which obtained at the time of the canonization, and had been promoted by factors which initially do not seem to have interested even the most interested of the petitioners.

For there can be little doubt that the driving force behind the successful presentation of King Edward's cause was the abbey of Westminster, in the person of its abbot, Laurence, who was determined to make a great occasion of its happy conclusion. On 13 October 1163 St Edward's body was elevated to a new shrine in the presence of the most distinguished company that could be gathered. Many writers say that the king was present, and this is the late Westminster tradition, which lists a notable assembly of English and Norman bishops and earls.[84] One medieval source believes that Aelred was the preacher at these splendid proceedings,[85] and this could perhaps have been the case, although it seems more probable that this opinion, like that of many modern writers who assert the fact, was based on a misunderstanding of the Rievaulx tradition. For Walter Daniel makes it clear that Aelred's part in the celebrations was the execution of a double literary commission for abbot Laurence, who was a relative of his. Laurence had worked hard at collecting the witnesses to Edward's life and miracles and these he gave to Aelred to write up in a new and definitive life of the saint.[86] He also asked him to compose a liturgical homily to be read at the Office on the saint's feast day.[87] Although the text of this is claimed to have existed in one or two old library catalogues, it is no longer to be found today.[88] On the other hand the new *Life of St Edward* was a great success and the number and diffusion of the manuscripts of it are a sign of its popularity throughout the Middle Ages.

In a prefatory letter addressed to Laurence of Westminster, Aelred refers to a single volume which he had received from the abbot, from the general tenor of which he has not departed, though he has added a few things from reliable chronicles and trustworthy tales of old men.[89] Upon examination it becomes clear that the new life is, in fact, firmly based on that of Osbert of Clare, the order and contents of whose chapters is closely followed. At the end Aelred adds five new miracle stories, two of which concern Osbert of Clare, and may have been recorded by him. Within the life itself Aelred inserts four new stories, two concerning the family of earl Godwin, and two whose picturesque character ensured their future repetition and popularity. One of these tells how Edward watches a thief stealing from the treasury in his bedchamber and encourages him to make good his escape before he is caught.[90] The other recounts how the king receives back from St John the Evangelist a ring he had given in alms in his honour.[91] This story determined the future iconography of Edward, who is shown in the Wilton Diptych and other medieval works of art holding a ring.

A more distinctly personal contribution of Aelred must be seen in connection with the prologue addressed to Henry II. A strange deathbed vision of king Edward, mentioned by earlier writers, including the unknown author of the first life, suggests to Aelred the possibility of a final vindication of all his work on royal genealogies. In this vision it had been revealed to the king that evil times would follow his death and, upon his asking when there would be a respite, he was told a parable. The top of a green tree is removed from the trunk and carried three acres away. If the severed part should return to the trunk and actually bear fruit, then better times can be expected. For both Osbert of Clare and William of Malmesbury, who quote them, these words, as expressing an impossibility, are a message of unmitigated gloom. For Aelred, they vindicate the king's claim to the gift of prophecy, and he feels confident of giving them an interpretation which refutes the views of previous writers.[92] The root from which the line of English kings comes is Alfred. With its once separated trunk restored, it bears fruit at last in Henry II. He is, in Aelred's words in his letter of dedication to the king, "the cornerstone", joining the Norman and English nations in his royal person. The specially divine sanction of that royal tradition is emphasized by reference to the story of the consecration of Alfred by the pope himself. How far these notions appealed to

Henry it is difficult to be sure, but of their importance for Aelred there can be no doubt. The need to find a satisfactory formula for the final reconciliation of feeling between Englishmen and Normans would seem more urgent to him. With the general picture of his kingly prerogatives which emerges from this work Henry cannot, however, have been displeased, though it may be noted that Aelred's *Life of Edward* cannot have done anything to promote a belief in the power of a King's touch, since it returns to the standpoint of the earliest life and insists that Edward's special gift was the curing of the blind.[93]

At another level, the new life which, as Walter Daniel says, was "brilliant for its literary excellence" may have taken the fancy of a king brought up in literary circles. Its whole texture is quite different from the baroque Latin of Osbert of Clare, writing twenty years earlier a language encrusted with classical allusions. In Aelred mannerisms of a new kind appear. Osbert had compared Edward to one of Plato's philosopher kings and his wife, Edith, to Minerva. For Aelred, who confines himself to the images of the scriptures, he is rather the peaceful Solomon, and Edith is "lovely of face, but lovelier in her moral integrity." The phrases which describe her would be appropriate to a nun in a house of reformed observance. We are told that like king David in his old age she was accustomed to read or work with her hands. Aelred's use of a regular, rhythmic Latin, such as the style in saints' lives now requires, helps to create an atmosphere suitable to people from whose lives all the roughnesses of daily living have been smoothed out. We miss the chuckle that Osbert permits his king. Aelred only allows him to break into a smile, "but keeping the kingly dignity". His kings live and move in a world of their own.

5

"God is Friendship"

If, in the world of the great, Aelred seems sometimes to walk a little like a wondering child, this is perhaps a reflection of his own earlier education and of the ardent idealism in which, by vocation, he was caught up. He had, after all, even as a boy, been admitted into a charmed circle, in which everything was strange and new and exciting; and later at Rievaulx, in a setting incomparably more austere, he had been drawn by claims of another kind still more intimately binding in their effect on his personality. As at court in the immediate circle of king David so, for all its differences, in the monastery, Aelred was accustomed to living with men who believed intensely in the worth of what they were doing. At Rievaulx, however, he had also learned by reflection and prayer to examine the motives of human action and to lay bare the processes of the heart so that, although he could discern human weakness as well as anyone, it became increasingly difficult for him to conceive how anyone could seriously want anything less than the ideal. We must believe that the doctrine of the *Mirror of Charity*—that the thirst of rational beings for true happiness can never be lost and that "there is no one who would not prefer to be sick in body rather than sick in mind"[1] —expresses a deep personal conviction. To be a man and not a beast, and to be aware that one is a man, is also to be aware of capacities of mind and heart which cry out for their fulfilment. It was these longings which Aelred found reawakened and strengthened by contact with those he most loved and admired. It does such a man no discredit that he sometimes thinks better of others than they fully deserve. For, just as he loses nothing by the generosity of his belief in them, so they gain a great deal by being made to feel that they ought not to fall below the level of their true selves. Like every born teacher, Aelred was instinctively aware of the formative value of relationships which produce effects like these. He had experienced it in his own life, and was ready to pass what he had learned on to others.

Looking back on his youth, after the years of reading and quiet that preceded his appointment as novice-master in 1142, Aelred saw that it was friendship that still held him back when already Waldef had taken the decision to put on the religious habit and that, when he too eventually chose a similar way of life, it was friendship in the cloister that had sustained and supported and instructed him. "The rule of our Order forbade us to speak", he says of his friend Simon, "but his face spoke to me, his bearing spoke to me, his silence talked."[2] Always it had been there, wilder and less discriminating perhaps, sudden and irrationally unpredictable, yet there instinctively, this love of people and this need to be loved, so that in the young Augustine of the *Confessions*[3] Aelred seemed to find himself.

When I was still a boy at school, and the charm of my school-fellows was my great delight, of the habits and faults which commonly trouble that age, it was mine to give myself wholly to affection and abandon myself to love, so that nothing seemed pleasanter, nothing more worth while than to love and be loved. Thus it came about that I was tossed hither and thither between changing loves and friendships and, not knowing the laws of true friendship, was often deceived by its counterfeit. At length the book which Cicero wrote on friendship one day fell into my hands and I was immediately taken by the value of its considered views and the beauty of its style. And, although I saw that friendships like those were not for me, still I was glad to have found a criterion of friendship by which to check the aberrations of my own loves and affections.[4]

With these words Aelred begins the prologue of the book on *Spiritual Friendship* which he himself eventually completed. The need for it was thus in many ways the oldest of his conscious spiritual needs, and probably even the plan of the book goes back a long way in his religious life. The third part of the *Mirror of Charity* had, in effect, been a treatise on the principles governing friendship. But in that work, as in the prologue and the first part of the book on *Spiritual Friendship*, Aelred records the initial reserve about Cicero and the pagan philosophers which he had felt when he became a novice and was plunged into reading the scriptures. In his first fervour he found that everything about his old life seemed to pall and even of Cicero on *Friendship* he says:

> I found to my surprise that it did not please me as it used. For then nothing that had not been sweetened with the honey of the beloved Jesus, nothing that was not seasoned with the salt of holy scripture could quite hold my heart.

But, as time went on, he was still haunted by this theme.

> And, turning it over again and again, I tried to discover if I could not perhaps give it a foundation in the authority of scripture. Desiring to love in a spiritual way, although I could not succeed, I decided, after I had read much about friendship in the writings of the holy Fathers, to write about spiritual friendship, and lay down for myself the rules of a pure and holy love.

To complete the work satisfactorily Aelred needed to feel entirely free to reconsider Cicero objectively in the light of the teaching of scripture and the Fathers. The finished work shows that in the end he discovered this boldness and in no other Christian adaptation of Cicero's teaching does so much of this source survive. The first part of Aelred's treatise is to some extent coloured by his earlier attitude, though he has there put his own former reserves into the mouth of his young friend Ivo, the monk of Wardon to whom the exposition of the gospel on *Jesus as a boy of twelve* had been sent.[5] At the beginning of the second part, Ivo is referred to as dead, and the discovery of the draft of the section in which he appears, leads to a reopening of the discussion. Walter Daniel, Aelred's biographer, is now one of the speakers. There is no reason to suppose that the lapse of time between the original conception and its final execution is a literary fiction. It needed the calmness of maturity and experience to carry the plan through, and an allusion to the anti-pope Paschal III in the second dialogue makes it clear that Aelred cannot have been putting the finishing touches to his book before the late spring of 1164,[6] when he had already long been burdened by ill-health and was often forced to withdraw from the stream of things to the little hut they had built for him, near the monastic infirmary.[7] Could he have known the circumstances in which Cicero had written his dialogue on *Friendship*, he would perhaps have felt a still greater affinity with him.

For the *Laelius*, as it was commonly called from the name of its principal speaker, the mouthpiece of Cicero's views, belongs to that final spurt of literary activity with which in the years 45–44 B.C. Cicero occupied and consoled himself in his country retreat against the thoughts of political disaster and the crippling blow of his daughter's death. The dialogue must have been written at considerable speed, but its atmosphere of reflective tranquillity is a tribute to all that Cicero's lifelong friendship with Atticus had meant to him. It was natural that this work with its picture of humane intercourse and its tone of high ethical idealism should have had a special appeal to a century that was rediscovering the same values. Aelred had evidently met it before he had any contact with the Cistercians, and a copy of it was among the books of the family friend Laurence of Durham.[8] Its importance for the common Cistercian doctrine of the spiritual life is readily recognizable, and although we do not know for certain if there was a copy in the library at Rievaulx, the nearby abbey of Byland certainly had one which still exists, and which shows signs of serious twelfth-century use.[9]

Cicero, who was probably more dependent on the Greek of Theophrastus than on any other classical source, has constructed his treatise in the form of a dialogue between three friends, and its discursive form makes it difficult to analyse systematically. Aelred shows every sign of having mastered it as a whole so that, although where he is most dependent upon Cicero the sequence of his ideas largely follows that of his source,[10] they have become familiar enough for him to manipulate them as he pleases in a discussion to which he has successfully given a personal and contemporary character. The division of the treatise into three books suggests the imposition of a simple scholastic plan upon the material, but there are inevitable repetitions and digressions in a work where the dialogue form of the model has been retained. The scheme, which is rather like that of the *Mirror of Charity*, to which indeed it forms a pendant, is however more evidently carried through than in the larger work. The first dialogue deals with the nature and origin of friendship, the second vindicates its value, and the third discusses its practice. Aelred evokes genuine scenes and characters and, especially in the two later books, the illusion of intimate and spontaneous discussion is created with some skill.

It emerges that the first conversation is taking place at the abbey of Wardon, where Aelred, as abbot of the mother house, is con-

8

ducting a visitation. On an occasion when everyone has something to say, Aelred has noticed the young Ivo silent in the background.

> One minute you raised your head, about to say something, but then you lowered it, as though your voice were stuck in your throat, and held your peace. After a bit, you left us, but you came back again, wearing a sad face. By all this you made me see that, when you want to say what is in your mind, you shun a crowd, and prefer privacy.

And so Aelred has thought of a way to give Ivo an opportunity to talk. The abbot's opening words, which go on to put Ivo at his ease, express in a sense the burden of the whole treatise and raise, by implication, the problem to be discussed in the first dialogue. "Here are you and I; and I hope Christ makes a third between us." But if this is true, how can it make sense to think that Cicero, whose book on *Friendship* Ivo, like Aelred, has known from his youth, can have anything to say to them? Can it possibly teach them, Ivo will want to know, how that friendship, which ought to exist between them, begins in Christ, is preserved for Christ, and has its purpose and value referred to him? "For it is clear that Cicero did not know the virtue of true friendship, since he was totally ignorant of its source and object, namely Christ." For the moment Aelred evades the force of this interesting question, so often discussed by Augustine, as to whether the pagans can have any real virtues at all,[11] and begins at once by quoting Cicero's definition of friendship and submitting it to examination. "Friendship is an accord in benevolence and charity on things human and divine."[12] Aelred understands Cicero to mean by "charity" the heart's affection, and by "benevolence" its expression in action. With some reluctance, Ivo agrees to accept this definition as a starting-point for their discussion. Aelred then introduces another dictum of Cicero, where he says that in Latin the word for "friend" is derived from the word for "love".[13] Aelred assumes that Ivo will be familiar with his exposition of the entire subject of love in the *Mirror of Charity*, and adds that a friend is said to be like the keeper of one's love or, as some would say, one's soul-keeper. His functions are, as far as possible, to cure, or at least to bear with, one's faults, and regard all that concerns one's good as his own. Hence friendship, as even the pagan philosophers agree, is not among the virtues that pass away, but among those that are everlasting. As scripture says: "He that is a friend loveth at all times",[14] and Jerome declares: "A friendship that can come to an end was never a true one."[15]

It is, then, Ivo retorts, no surprise how rare a thing friendship is. He recalls Cicero remarking that antiquity preserves the memory of only about three or four pairs of friends,[16] and feels that if, even in Christian times, friendship is so rare, it is perhaps because it is too noble a thing for most people to aim at. "But it is already a great thing to attempt great things", Aelred replies, and it does one no harm to be aware of how far short of one's ideals one falls. Further, a Christian, who so often hears the words: "Ask and you shall receive", ought not to despair of being heard on this matter too. Did not the first Christians, of whom it was said that they were of one mind and heart and did not call anything their own, satisfy Cicero's definition of what friendship is? This is a leading question, for the citation of the verse from the Acts of the Apostles, which is so important for John Cassian's theory of the primitive origins of the monastic life, is also a reminder of how intimately the doctrine of friendship and the doctrine of Christian perfection are linked in Aelred's mind. Unlike many later spiritual writers, Aelred belongs to a tradition which finds the cloister, where accord on so many basic matters can be assumed, to be a natural setting for the development of friendship. Far from being an enemy of perfection, friendship is a sign of spiritual health. Aelred cites the case of the martyrs as being the primary exponents of this generous Christian love, and mentions a tale told by Ambrose in his treatise on *Virgins*, "which I think you have often read, not without tears." Thus tradition and authority witness to the truth of the saying of Christ that "greater love than this no man has, that a man lay down his life for his friends".

The question then arises: Are friendship and charity the same thing? This is evidently not the case, since we are bound to love even our enemies, but only to our friends can we commit without fear our hearts and what is in them. Nor would it be right to extend the name of friend to those who are united in vice. For that man does not really love who loves evil, and he who loves evil does not love but, as the psalmist says, "hates his own soul". Hating the true interests of his own soul, how can he love those of anyone else? Yet it is true that one could speak of a certain carnal friendship, which consists in liking and disliking the same things. "This is the kind of friendship which is entered into without reflection, never submitted to sound judgement or ruled by reason, swept on through everything by the impulse of feeling, knowing no moderation, seeking nothing worthy, not troubling about fitting and unfitting, but going about all it does thoughtlessly, imprudently, capriciously, and unrestrainedly." It is the kind of relationship which is dropped as easily as it was begun. There is, too, another worldly kind of friendship which is governed simply by self-interest. It is always full of deceptions and uncertainties, depending, as it does, upon temporary mutual advantages.

> But the spiritual friendship which we call genuine is sought, not with an eye on any worldly expediency, or for some ulterior motive, but simply on account of its own natural worth and the inclination of the human heart, so that its profit and its reward is nothing other than itself. Thus the Lord in the Gospel says: "I have appointed you that you should go and should bring forth fruit", that is, should love one another. For in true friendship one travels by making progress, and receives the fruit in the experience of the delight of its perfection. Thus spiritual friendship is begotten between the good, who have lives, habits, and interests that are alike, which is "accord in benevolence and charity on things human and divine". So this definition seems to me to be adequate to express the notion of friendship if, however, according to our usage, we understand "charity" to exclude from friendship everything vicious.

In this justification of Cicero's definition of friendship Aelred explicitly alludes to that note of disinterestedness in love which so much appealed to the early Cistercian writers as an essential way of insisting upon the worthwhileness of Christian love in itself.[17] When he goes on to speak of the origin and source of friendship, Aelred makes it quite clear that this disinterestedness in love, which is a reflection of God's disinterested self-giving in creation, is in no sense incompatible with a genuine sense of need. God alone is unneedy; only to him every creature cries: "Thou art my God, for thou hast no need of my goods." Everything else needs the completion of relationship for its fulfilment in a world in which a vestige of God's own supreme unity has been left in the natural tendency of all things to fall into an order in time and place. From stones in the brook and trees in the wood to animals at play, everything seems to long for companionship. Cicero had also observed this apparently universal reflection of the rational desire for union of like with like,[18] which the Fall has not destroyed. It is, however, the result of Original Sin that the charity in which man was created, which was in a certain sense "natural" to him, has grown cold. The private good is now sought over against the common good, and avarice and envy encroach upon friendship. In this state of things it has become necessary to distinguish between charity and friendship. Even the most perverse have to be loved, but it is clear that there cannot be any community of will and opinion between the good and the evil. It is true that the natural desire for friendship shows signs of survival even among the most self-seeking of the pursuers of wealth or pleasure, such is the persistence of the condition in which man was created. But the reality of friendship has been forced to withdraw to the circle of those who have that genuine accord which is only possible to the good. To say this is to say that friendship is as natural to man as the virtues are, not in the sense that everyone has the virtues, but in the sense that they constitute man's normal, human perfection, and hence deserve to be the object of our efforts. Aelred then quotes an Augustinian principle which is, in effect, his only answer to the problem as to whether Cicero or any other pagan philosopher could have experienced what true friendship was. It is a notion often referred to in the development of scholastic moral theory that a virtue is a quality which the man who has it uses rightly and which no one at all abuses.[19] Aelred, like his contemporaries, still lacks the equipment to unravel all the subtle implications of this view but, with the aid of a verbal citation from a sermon of Augustine,[20] he sufficiently answers Ivo's objection that it is obvious that many people do in fact abuse the virtues they possess. Augustine is speaking of wisdom, but his words apply to any other virtue as well. His point is that, to the extent to which a man's action reveals his lack of a given virtue, to that extent he cannot be said to possess it, and consequently cannot abuse it, since the virtues, when used, are always concerned with virtuous action. They are also always inevitably related to each other so that, for instance, a proud chastity cannot really be a virtue. This manifest interrelation even between quite distinct virtues is, Aelred believes, his justification for assimilating friendship so closely to wisdom. When Cicero's definition of friendship is taken in combination with the authority of scripture and of Jerome, it is seen to have about it the notes of love, truth and perpetuity, and are these not the characteristics of wisdom? Delighted with this suggestion, Ivo is emboldened to ask whether, arguing along the same lines, one might not be justified in saying, on the basis of the most familiar of all St John's sayings, that "God is friendship". Aelred hesitates before an expression consecrated neither by use nor authority, but he is prepared to agree that one could certainly say of friendship that "he who abides in friendship, abides in God and God in him". With this synthesis of philosophical theory and evangelical doctrine the first dialogue closes on a note of satisfaction.

The presumption is that the second dialogue begins at Rievaulx after a considerable lapse of time, and on this occasion a third character, Gratian, is introduced to act as a foil for the nervous, ironic, intelligent Walter, whose personality is depicted with several lifelike touches. Walter Daniel tells us in his *Life of Aelred* that it was he himself whom Aelred has thus portrayed.[21] It is not impossible that he was indeed the stimulus for giving a final literary form to a project long abandoned among the claims and stresses of a busy life. For one is often aware how much fidelity to his own views in life and action determined both what Aelred attempted and achieved. The work itself, in this case, shows unmistakable signs that, once he had finally given his mind to it, there can have been nothing nearer to Aelred's heart to do really well. In many ways it is the most finished, the most clearly argued, and the most charming of his writings, a testament to the deepest of his convictions.

The theoretical basis of the discussion up to this point is resumed by reference to the belief which Aelred shares with Cicero that "there is nothing more advantageous to seek in human affairs, nothing harder to find, nothing sweeter to experience" than friendship. It is not merely that, as scripture says, "a faithful friend is the medicine of life". It is also that, as a consequence, friendship is a step towards that perfection "which consists in the love and knowledge of God; so that, from being a friend of man, a man becomes a friend of God, according to that saying of our Saviour in the Gospel: 'I will not now call you my servants, but my friends'". It is, Aelred explains to the eager Gratian, precisely because in friendship everything is open, true and free that the soul grows in genuine Christian love. "And so a friend cleaving to his friend in the spirit of Christ becomes one heart and soul with him and thus, rising by the steps of love to the friendship of Christ, is made one spirit with him in one kiss."

In thus transposing Cicero's notion of union in friendship into the scriptural love language of the *Song of Songs*, Aelred introduces an ingenious adaptation of an important passage of Augustine's commentary on Genesis to help him explain the real significance of the kiss.[22] "The life of man", Aelred says, "is sustained by two sorts of nourishment, food and air, and a man can live for some time without food, but without air, not one single hour." The play on the word which means both "air" and "spirit" in Latin cannot be reproduced in English, but it must be understood in the sentence in which Aelred says that "in a kiss two spirits meet and mix and are united". Then, like Augustine writing about Genesis, who says that there are three kinds of prophetic vision, Aelred says there are three kinds of kiss, a bodily kiss, a spiritual kiss, and a mental kiss. "The bodily kiss is made by the impression of the lips, the spiritual kiss by the union of souls, the mental kiss by the spirit of God in the infusion of graces." The bodily kiss can only be offered or received for definite and upright reasons for, like water and fire, which are in themselves good, this natural sign of true love can be misused. It is the spiritual kiss which is really proper to friendship. "It is given, not by the touch of the mouth, but by the affection of the heart." Since, when it is right, the love which inspires this affection is God's gift, it may be said to be Christ who kisses us in this affection, "not with his own mouth, but with another's". It is this experience which deepens in the soul its longing for Christ himself and makes it cry out, with the spouse in the *Song of Songs*, "Let him kiss me with the kiss of his mouth".

This mystical flight, not unexpectedly, rather frightens the young Gratian, who declares that he had not hitherto thought of friendship as being connected with anything quite so exalted, and had always regarded it rather as a certain capacity for mutual accommodation. Walter agrees that there is a real need to discuss in rather more practical terms what the real limitations of friendship are. Aelred replies that Christ himself has laid down its measure in saying that "greater love than this no man has, that a man lay down his life for his friends". But, asks the persistent Walter, shall we say that evil men and pagans who reach the point of feeling prepared to die for each other, have reached the fullness of friendship? This Aelred will not allow, for he insists that true friendship can only arise between the good, grow between those who are making spiritual progress, and reach its fullness between the perfect. In other words, as he has earlier explained, as the stepping-stone to maturity in the life of charity, friendship follows the same pattern as the traditional

threefold division of the spiritual life into the condition of those
who are beginning, those who are progressing, and those who are
perfect. It is, indeed, only an aspect of this spiritual growth. Hence
the view that one should do anything he asks to please a friend is
to be rejected with abhorrence. "It is no excuse for a sin, if you
do it for a friend." There is no special difficulty in showing that
friendship between men who cannot depend upon each other's
uprightness cannot survive.

Gratian finds the sound of these exacting ideals hardly less de-
pressing for his own prospects than the former spiritual perspectives
which seemed to pass beyond his grasp. Aelred hastens to reassure
him that he is far from supposing that only men who are almost
perfect are good. But Walter will not be encouraged, and feels it
would be safer to avoid a path so full of cares. Aelred can only
retort with Cicero that "those who take friendship out of life, would
seem to take the sun out of the world".[23] After all, there is no virtue
that can be acquired without some pains. "I would say that they
are not so much men as beasts who say that one should live without
being a comfort to anyone, taking no delight in another's good,
causing no trouble to others by one's faults, loving no one, and
caring to be loved by no one. Yet heaven forbid I should allow them
really to love who think friendship is a business affair, only pro-
fessing to be friends with their lips when the hope of some temporal
advantage smiles on them, or who try to make their friends the
minister of some vile practice." Aelred thus dismisses mercenary
and what he calls "puerile" friendships, which are all emotion and
unregulated feeling, and insists that "that man has not yet learned
what friendship is, who wants of it any other reward than itself".
The love of David and Jonathan did, in fact, bring tangible benefits to both, but the friendship in which their union was grounded,
was entered into for the sake of virtue itself and preceded any hope
of future advantages.

In this estimate of the ascetic and spiritual value of friendship
Aelred has doubtless set his sights deliberately high. In the third
dialogue, like the friends of whom he writes, he at last unbends
to the more immediate and practical concerns of his questioners.
"The source and origin of friendship is love, for there cannot be
love without friendship, or friendship ever without love." But, as
the previous discussions have already implied, love has different
causes. Using again the analysis of the third book of the *Mirror of*

Charity,[24] Aelred suggests that the source of love may be in nature itself, as in family ties, or in some kind of service given and received which creates a relationship. It can further be based on considerations of reason alone as, to quote the extreme case, our love of our enemies is, or on feeling alone, as when we are drawn to someone simply by their physical beauty, their strength, or their fair speech. Finally, friendship can arise from a combination of these factors of respect and attraction. Obviously the last makes for the most satisfactory kind of friendship, but Gratian wishes to know whether we can, in fact, always admit to our friendship people who appear to qualify for it in this way. Aelred insists that the only solid foundation for friendship is the love of God, "to which everything which love or affection suggests, everything to which hidden inclination or the overt proposition of a friend urges us, should be referred". But it is further necessary to realize that we cannot make a friend of everybody we love, for all are not suitable for anything so intimate. Friendship must be stable and so, if it is to lead to that accord about things human and divine which the true nature of friendship requires, it must result from careful choice and a sensible period of probation, before one opens oneself entirely to its possibilities. There are, for instance, some kinds of defects of character which make it difficult for a man to be true to a friendship for long. One clearly has to be careful about choosing for one's friends the irascible, the unstable, the suspicious, the talkative. This is not to say that one cannot find ways of dealing with such people and helping them to overcome their faults. A highly irascible friend of Aelred is alluded to during the conversation. With such men, one must give oneself time, as Aelred has in this case, to discover that one is capable of nullifying the risks which relationships with them always involve. The real solvents of friendship are constant reproofs, pride, the disclosing of secrets, treachery, as the book of Ecclesiasticus says.[25] It is, then, necessary to choose for one's friend a man of like habits and temperament. For, as Ambrose says, "there can be no friendship between people of different character".[26]

Where, then, to find such a friend? Aelred declares that the best kind of friend to make is the man who is growing all the time by overcoming his faults in the constant practice of the virtues, and is all the more reliable for the kind of maturity which comes from having temptations and difficulties and being used to dealing with them steadily. Naturally, if faults, either against oneself or against those one has reason to love as well, manifest themselves after the period of trial in friendship, everything possible must be done to correct them. Should a break nevertheless be inevitable, the relationship should if possible, as Cicero says, be "gently unsewn".[27] In a friend fidelity, intention, discretion, and patience have to be proved, for these are necessary for that gradual growth in virtue which friendship exists to foster. This is the reason why it is essential to beware of that impulse of love which runs ahead of sound judgement. In affection one ought to move forward step by step, until one is really ready to give oneself.

Gratian still retains a little of the view of those who think that all this is too exacting, and Aelred proceeds to a new defence of the worthwhileness of friendship. It is actually a foretaste of heaven, "where no one hides his thoughts or disguises his affection. This is that true and everlasting friendship, which begins here and is perfected there. Here, few know it, where few are good. There, everyone shares it, where all are good". Even in this world, where not all we love can be our friends, how much easier it is to live in an atmosphere of love and trust, rather than surrounded by every kind of suspicion, loving no one and feeling oneself to be loved by no one.

> The day before yesterday, when I was going round the cloister of the monastery, sitting with the brethren in a loving circle, as though amid the delights of paradise, I admired the leaves, the flowers, and the fruits of every tree. I found no one in that great number whom I did not love, and whom I did not believe loved me. I was filled with such a joy as passes all the delights of this world. For I felt as though my spirit were transfused into them all, and their affection into me, so that I could say with the prophet: "Behold how good and how pleasant it is for brethren to dwell together in unity".

Yet the delights of friendship imply a greater intimacy than this, "for a friend hides nothing", as Ambrose says.[28] "How many we love to whom it would not be wise thus to open our souls and display our feelings, since their age, their understanding, or their judgement would not know how to bear it." Walter and Gratian feel that Aelred's ideals are too high for them and that their situation is nearer that of the youthful friendships described by Augustine in the *Confessions*, which consisted in talking and being merry together and doing each other pleasant services.[29] Aelred by no means rejects this as a beginning, when there is nothing untoward about it, and there are even signs that it might eventually develop into something more serious. Indeed, all his lengthy concluding remarks on the practice of friendship, which emphasize openness, cheerfulness, and equality, have the effect of relaxing the sense of effort, which his insistence on virtue has perhaps built up, and introduce the note of delicate, mutual courtesy which makes friendship a joy. As he talks Aelred finds himself full of reminiscences of the past, and the sun is already going down in the sky when he resumes what he has been saying.

> The first thing is to purify oneself, allowing oneself nothing that is not right, withdrawing oneself from nothing that is profitable. Loving oneself thus, one must love one's neighbour too, according to the same rule. But because love has gathered so many together here in this place, one must choose from among them a man to admit to the secrets of friendship by the law of familiarity.

These two can help each other, console each other, pray for each other.

And so, praying to Christ for his friend, and longing to be heard by Christ for his friend's sake, he reaches out with devotion and desire to Christ himself. And suddenly and insensibly, affection passing into affection, as though touched by the gentleness of Christ close at hand, he begins to taste how sweet he is and to feel how lovely he is. Thus, from that holy love with which he embraces his friend, he rises to that by which he embraces Christ.

It is, as it were, only a step to heaven where God is all in all.

All that lies behind the work on *Spiritual Friendship* can never be known to us, but its significance for Aelred's life must run through every year of it, giving a hidden meaning to all its eventualities. It is clearly linked to the deepest of his personal problems, and his stability in striving for their solution, and in helping others to do so too, is a mark of an uncommon bravery of spirit.

6

The Claims of the North

Public events provided Aelred with the appropriate occasion to acknowledge his debt to King David of Scotland, and the book on *Spiritual Friendship*, completed so late in his life, is the best memorial to the hidden and unbroken support of friends, chiefly within the monastery of Rievaulx, most of whom are unknown to us even by name. The ties of home and the claims of the life of the Church in Aelred's own northern England are represented by another group of writings which span the immensely active and creative years of his abbacy. Three of these are not mentioned by Walter Daniel, and there may well have been others of a minor character, like the jingle written in honour of St Cuthbert,[1] which have been lost in the debris of the past.

The final shape Aelred intended to give a collection of miracle stories connected with the relics and old churches of Hexham is, indeed, not quite clear from the manuscripts in which it survives. But, although much of it is unequal to his best writing, that the work is authentically his is attested by the old library catalogue of Rievaulx[2] whose manuscript of it, damaged in an eighteenth-century fire, still exists. Its condition permits verification, within limits, of its relation to other copies that were made of it.[3] It would seem that the nucleus of the book *On the miracles of the holy Fathers who rest in Hexham church*[4] is a sermon Aelred preached at Hexham on 3 March 1155, when the bones in which his father and uncle had interested themselves were translated to new shrines.[5] Aelred was the obvious preacher to choose for such an occasion, and what he had to say both then, and in the compilation he subsequently wove about his original discourse, is enlivened by personal reminiscences and observations. Without it some of his family history would be more difficult to write. He speaks not only of what he personally remembers but also of what he was told, and much of this belongs to a world very different from that in which he was writing and speaking. It is thus that once the elegant, rhythmic form of the opening sermon finally breaks down, disjointed as these stories often are, they have a peculiar interest for that period of transition and assimilation of which the very notion of the translation is a reminder. Even where no miracles occur, the bones of the past are, after all, not so easily disposed of, and in the world from which Aelred had come this fact was acknowledged by a sense of the presence of great and holy men so direct and physical as to be shocking to our very different sensibilities. Aelred is talking a very sophisticated, ecclesiastical language when in his sermon he tells us that "'just men shall live in everlasting remembrance', whose bones, even though dead, burgeon with frequent miracles from their resting-place, and whose memory which the years had buried or negligence destroyed, does not fail to continue with manifest signs". But, in the stories he tells, he is speaking the language his father and grandfather and the ordinary people of Hexham would have understood. These are folk tales with all their vivid crudeness and violence. Aelred's version of the rescue of Hexham by Wilfrid and Cuthbert from the threat of one of the terrible border raids of king Malcolm is an excellent illustration of this.[6] We see the desperate people of the little town gathered in the church praying to their local patrons. That night, the priest has a vision of two mounted bishops, who ride up and ask for fodder for their mares. The priest bewails the people's plight, but is calmly reassured that all has been arranged and that it will be impossible for the Scots to cross the river in the morning. When challenged, the speaker replies: "I am called Wilfrid,* and behold, this one with me is St Cuthbert, whom I fetched as I passed through Durham, so that coming together to our brethren who rest in this church we might preserve both their resting-place and their people." There could be no more telling way of expressing the sense of the continued interest of a saint in the place of his former labours. The people can go on to him, as Aelred says, "as though he were living".[7] The church where the bodies of the saints rest is the centre of the life of

---

* St Wilfrid's body was not at Hexham, but at Ripon.

the local people or "nation". In this particular case they are the sole
defence of an undefended city, and such immunity as the small
township enjoys in the frequent border skirmishes is due to them
as the originators of the traditional rights of sanctuary,[8] and as the
workers of miracles of sharp rebuke against evil-doers. Thus, on
more than one occasion, we are told of people in distress who lift
their eyes towards the church which can be seen clearly from all
points along the river-bank.

The saints repay all this devotion by an equally tenacious attachment to the people. The bodies of St Alchmund and St Eata thus
became, we are told, too heavy to be moved anywhere else. The
first incident results in the restoration of a stolen fragment,[9] the
second in the frustration of the efforts of archbishop Thomas II of
York to move the saint's body into "foreigner's country",[10] where
they were not so fortunate in such treasures. A slightly more unusual miracle story connected with attempted theft is told of Aelred's
uncle Aldred, the former Hexham shrine-keeper. When he
approaches the relics with the intention of taking away a portion,
he finds them as hot as a furnace.[11]

The Virgin of these anecdotes shares the somewhat fierce and
even vindictive character of the lesser holy ones. In Aelred's
sermons for her feast days she is normally the humble, obedient
handmaid, the "Mother of Mercy" of that new and tender devotion
which was taking Europe captive. But here at Hexham her older,
imperial dignity asserts itself when a sacrilegious Galloway soldier
takes a stone to break the lock of the round church Wilfrid had
dedicated to her, and for his pains the young barbarian is driven
out of his mind by a devil and dies, leaving his body as food for the
birds and beasts.[12] We need not doubt that Aelred transmits these
stories substantially as they came to him. Some he may owe to a
projected work on the same subject planned, but never executed,
by Richard of Hexham,[13] some details may even have been culled
from Bede,[14] but it is more than likely that most of them come from
the storehouse of his own family tradition. Once he appeals to his
own boyhood memory in support of an assertion,[15] but he is unfortunately more modest in mentioning the witness of his own eyes
than we could wish. Of the buildings or the people of Hexham, as
he knew them when he was young, perhaps only the old lay
brother of the priory, affectionately known as "bearded Hugh",
who was cured of a hernia, seems almost to come to life.[16] It is, on

the other hand, the imaginative power of the stories he has inherited that Aelred preserves within a tradition quite different from
that in which they had originated.

For the work *On the Miracles of Hexham Church* attempts to do
for Hexham the sort of thing that Goscelin of St Bertin had been
doing more than sixty years previously in connection with the
post-Conquest re-building and reconstruction at Canterbury.[17] The
need was universally felt. William of Malmesbury, speaking of the
relics of the saints with which St Ethelwald had filled the church
at Thorney, says that he will refrain from mentioning their names,
not only because they will sound barbarous and even amusing to
modern ears, but also because "it would seem to be frivolous if you
proclaim the merits of those about whom one cannot find any
miracle-books.[18] The Hexham saints laboured under a similar disadvantage. Their early lives had disappeared among the books from
the library established by Wilfrid and Acca, which the Danish invasions had destroyed, and a visiting cleric laughed to hear them
referred to as saints, when their names could not be found in any
recognized martyrology.[19] Aelred, whose family roots were in an
old English past, would do for his local saints what Goscelin of
St Bertin, a monk from abroad, had done so memorably for the
saints whose names had been venerated in pre-Norman Canterbury.
At Hexham, however, the local traditions were sturdy enough to
resist the refinements of the new style in hagiography and, if he
ever intended to do so, Aelred never quite smoothed down the
rough edges of the materials that had come his way. The old, simple,
wooden shrines in the church were replaced by new ones covered
with gold and silver and decorated with jewels, but Aelred's work
about the saints whose relics they contained never reached such a
degree of polished elaboration.

The case was quite different with another commission he must
have executed about the same time, or rather later. Walter Daniel
does not mention that Aelred's re-writing of the life of St Edward
the Confessor was not his only undertaking of this kind. The
Rievaulx catalogue knows of another, and again its text has survived. Aelred's prologue to his *Life of St Ninian*[20] indicates that he
had been officially asked to write it, evidently by one of the bishops
of Ninian's old see of Whithorn, which had been revived in or
about 1128 by Fergus of Galloway. The finished work, one of
Aelred's most purely literary compositions, is written in the rhythmic

Latin whose technique, in spite of his frequent assertions of lack of schooling, Aelred had certainly mastered by his middle years.[21] On this, and on other grounds, it is probable that his patron was Christian, the second bishop of the revived see, who had been consecrated at Bermondsey in December 1154, and eventually finished his days in the Cistercian house of Holm Cultrum.

The book is a short one, and Aelred must have had a rather free hand in writing it, for even Bede, whose few, carefully chosen words Aelred quotes,[22] had little trustworthy information about events so obscure and distant, and was evidently reading back into the past a view of Ninian's achievements which is anachronistic. Aelred's prologue refers to an additional source written in a "barbaric tongue", but a comparison with two poems on Ninian, written by pupils of Alcuin, shows that Aelred must mean, not a vernacular source, but one written in awkward, archaic Latin, whose information he shares in common with them.[23] Of the details peculiar to Aelred, it may be that the names of Aedelfridus and Deisuit, who were cured by Ninian's relics, derive from the lost life, as well as the account of the origin of the place name Farres Last. The story of the boy who tried to evade punishment by escaping to sea in a coracle also needs to be explained.

For the rest, Aelred's work reflects as faithfully as its literary form twelfth-century interests and a twelfth-century point of view. Ninian had been a simple missionary, and Aelred's picture of him as the founder of a diocese divided into parishes is inspired by the desire to discover in the past a justification for the ecclesiastical re-organization characteristic of the reign of King David of Scotland. Bede had mentioned Ninian's white church, after which his see had been called in Latin *Candida Casa*. Aelred links this remarkable building in stone with St Martin of Tours, from whose region he tells us Ninian brought his masons. The idea may have been suggested simply by Sulpicius Severus' *Life of St Martin* which, like all his contemporaries, Aelred knew so well, but he could have had some independent tradition on the subject. Certainly the talk of the people who asserted that they could remember kings in the region where Ninian was born is a reminder of the very real undercurrent of contemporary difficulties which David had had to face when he became king.

The *Life of St Ninian* is the work of a meticulous and sophisticated author at his desk, but Aelred never lived habitually in so tranquil a world. The needs of souls, disputes between monasteries, and the difficulties that arose within them, constantly called him away. As late as 1164 he was at Kirstead in Lincolnshire to sign an agreement between the Cistercians and the founder of the only English religious Order, Gilbert of Sempringham, determining the relation between the granges of the respective communities and other matters likely to lead to trouble.[24] Gilbert, whose Order had grown out of the counselling of young women, had always been on friendly terms with the Cistercians and in 1147, the year in which Aelred became abbot of Rievaulx, he had actually gone to the Cistercian general chapter, in the hope that it would assume control of his communities. The Cistercians were, however, still reluctant to have anything to do with the government of women.[25] Nor need it be assumed that it was only the fear of the kind of incident on which Aelred eventually wrote a long report that determined their decision. For the reputation of the Gilbertine nuns stood extremely high throughout the century and even Aelred's unpleasant tale is prefaced by remarks to the same effect. The attitude of Cîteaux was doubtless determined rather by considerations of time and an awareness of the special psychological problems involved.

Nevertheless it was natural that St Gilbert should call in Aelred to investigate a curious case which occurred in one of his many double monasteries of nuns and canons, probably sometime about 1160. The Cistercian Henry Murdac, elected and confirmed Archbishop of York in 1147, had entrusted a girl of about four to the nuns of the Gilbertine monastery of Watton in Yorkshire. Since Henry had died in 1154 this girl cannot have reached the age of puberty much before 1160. She then began to show herself incorrigibly unsuitable for convent life, formed an attachment to one of the canons, and became pregnant. Livid at this affront to their reputation, the nuns beat her unmercifully and clapped her feet in irons. The young canon having taken flight, his brethren decided to decoy him at night by disguising one of their number with a veil and, catching the unfortunate youth by this means, they administered a sound thrashing. Then the nuns, "having the zeal of God, but not according to knowledge", found some pretext for persuading the canons to hand their victim over. Dragging him into the presence of the imprisoned girl, they thrust a knife into his hands and forced him to mutilate himself. It was then that the dead

9

archbishop intervened and, appearing to the girl in sleep, told her to recite psalms. The pregnancy, to the amazement of the community, disappeared and even one fetter fell off. At this point Aelred was called in. He counselled that they should await the course of events and when, after his visit, the second fetter fell away, he felt able to say that a matter which God had evidently settled ought to remain closed.

Only one copy of Aelred's account of the story of *the Nun of Watton* survives,[26] and it is not its unsavoury details which make it worthy of notice. It is rather Aelred's insistence that this was a convent where

> in the midst of daily manual labour and the customary chanting of the psalms, the nuns were devoted to spiritual duties and visited by heavenly contemplations, so that many of them, as if bidding farewell to the world and the things of this world, were often rapt in unspeakable ecstasies and seemed to assist the angelic choirs.

There must be an element of exaggeration in this view, coloured as it is by the conventional language of piety, but it is nevertheless possible that Aelred is really only unconsciously drawing our attention to one of those strange contradictions which are so often to be found in religious history. We share his relief at not having to worry himself any further with women beneath whose lives of prayer a primitive barbarity only slumbered.

Especially in the last four years of his life, when such affairs did not require his attention, Aelred more and more withdrew to the inner oratory of his little hut near the infirmary.[27] What this little hut had meant for him imaginatively all through the last ten years of his life, Walter Daniel does not suggest. At the beginning of the long letter on the *Life of Recluses*, written for his sister during these years of semi-retirement, Aelred says that he is her "brother in the flesh and in the spirit".[28] By this he may intend no more than to refer to their common dedication to the service of God. But to William of St Thierry to whom, it is true, this notion made a special, personal appeal, all the monks of Clairvaux were "solitaries",[29] and Aelred too may have had a feeling of special affinity with his sister's vocation to the life of solitude. In the world from which Aelred came this vocation was widely accepted and honoured, and no account of the religious life of the north of England in his day which only mentioned the features of change and the occasional troubles and scandals would be complete. There was a long continuity behind the attraction to the eremitical life. Not only had the great St Cuthbert finished his life in solitude, but so had many others both before and since his day. In the eighth century St John of Beverley had used a little anchorage just across the Tyne from Hexham. The Durham book of benefactors, which goes back to the ninth century, originally listed its donors in order of dignity, and in those lists the hermits come immediately after the kings and queens and before the abbots.[30] At the time Aelred was writing, a Durham monk, Bartholomew, was once again living as a hermit on Cuthbert's Farne islands. But a closer and more personal contact was with the colourful Godric of Finchale, a friend and confidant of Aelred, who was instrumental in getting Godric's life written by Reginald of Durham. From this life we learn that Godric had his sister Burcwen living in an anchorhold close at hand which he had himself built for her. She was evidently not completely enclosed, since she was able to attend Mass in Godric's oratory when he had a priest staying with him,[31] as Aelred sometimes did. Of Aelred's own sister we know neither her name, nor the place where her cell was. We should expect it to be somewhere in the area between Hexham and Durham, most probably in a churchyard, but there were women with an attraction to solitude near York too and, when Aelred was still a young man, Archbishop Thurston had tried to persuade a notable recluse, Christina of Markyate near St Albans, to come and take charge of his newly-founded community of nuns.[32] She preferred to continue in solitude, but even there such women were neither isolated nor deprived of spiritual influence. Aelred's sister had, according to his own confession, waited a long time for him to write something for her, and was an anchoress of experience by the time she received a work which she had requested not just for herself, but for other younger women, whom she had encouraged to embrace this form of life, and to whom she was having to give counsel. Aelred was thus ensured of an audience of more than one, and in fact his work never ceased altogether to have some influence on English anchoresses throughout the Middle Ages.[33]

Walter Daniel places the *Life of Recluses* between the writing of the book on *Spiritual Friendship* and the *Life of St Edward*.[34] All these dates are clearly meant to be only approximate and it is even probable that all three works were being written simultaneously in the years 1163-4. So alike are they in form and spirit that it is

difficult not to believe that the *Life of Recluses* has been profoundly
affected by one of the most influential of all Jerome's letters, that on
virginity addressed to Eustochium, the daughter of St Paula.[35]
Fundamentally Aelred's work too is an ascetic letter on the preservation of virginity, which incorporates a Benedictine timetable and
dietary, together with some glowing advice on how to meditate.
An examination of his sources shows that, when Aelred tells us
vaguely that he has drawn his notions "from the ordinances of
different Fathers", he means chiefly Jerome, Ambrose, Gregory,
and Augustine rather than specifically monastic legislators. Nor
shall we be altogether taken in by the conventional avowal of tread-
ing the path of tradition. In this highly original treatise there are
very few phrases that can be cited as direct quotation, and the influence of monastic rules, apart from that of St Benedict, or of
contemporary directives for leading the eremitical life, would seem
to be negligible. It is sufficient to compare Aelred's letter with the
lucid and delightful ninth-century *Rule for Solitaries* of Grimlac[36]
to appreciate the contrast with a work which is formally planned as
a rule. How many hermits ever lived by the prescriptions of Grimlac we are not in a position to say, but it would evidently be an
illusion to suppose that even in the first half of the twelfth century
a properly codified rule was always adopted. The *Life of Recluses*,
like many works of its kind, is thus written in the form of an
admonitory letter, which bears in mind the dangers of the in-
experienced and the needs of beginners in the life of prayer. Broadly
speaking the letter falls into two unequal halves,[37] of which the first
and shorter is mainly devoted to the discussion of "bodily things",
the anchoress's relations with the outside world, her clothes and her
diet, the division and occupation of her time. The second, which
contains Aelred's most original ideas, is more specifically about
"spiritual things" to which the regular observances are naturally
ordained.

Aelred's brief opening statement of the various reasons for em-
barking upon a life of solitude draws a traditional distinction
between those solitaries who live at large in the desert, maintaining
themselves by the work of their own hands, and those who restrict
their restless tendencies still further by shutting themselves up in a
cell. Unlike Peter Damian, however,[38] Aelred does not appropriate
a special name to each class, and he refers to his sister both as a
"recluse" and an "anchoress".[39] With characteristic skill Aelred very

quickly passes to a lively discussion of the prevalent abuses which militate against the very purpose of enclosure. There are, apparently, many women who, although shut up in a cell, might just as well be wandering about the town all day, prying into the affairs of everyone who comes to market. The tone is that of the satirist.

> Nowadays you will scarcely find a single recluse alone, before whose window a talkative old woman or a gossip is not sitting; someone who will be keeping her busy with tales, feeding her on rumours and detractions, describing the appearance, the face and deportment of this or that monk, clerk, or religious, throwing in a spicy anecdote or two, telling of the infatuations of young girls, the license of widows to do what they please, the ingenuity of wives in deceiving their husbands and satisfying their desires (par 2).

It is scarcely surprising that, when at last she is left to herself, an anchoress whose imagination has been fired with this kind of talk is confused at her Office, gets no light from her reading, and cannot concentrate on her prayers. Often the cell eventually becomes a common brothel. This is strong language, if we are to suppose, as Aelred could be taken to imply, that what he says is based on generally received report. But it is only the first and gravest danger to the recluse's purpose. It is likely that we are closer to the commoner state of affairs in the portrait of the anchoress whose energies are devoted to doing business in a small way by keeping sheep or cattle and who, on the ever available pretext of needing to give alms, yields to the insidious temptation to become a money-grubber. "This is why things must be so arranged that the mind is relieved of all worldly cares and unburdened of every anxiety."

The anchoress may either support herself by the work of her own hands, a practice to which Aelred gives his Cistercian preference, or she may arrange, before she is enclosed, to receive from some benefactor just what is necessary for her bare daily sustenance. "But you sit, you keep silence, you suffer things to happen" (par 4). The phrase breaks in like an incantation, drawing the mind away from the world of chatter and commerce. People will quickly come to know that a woman who has yielded herself exclusively to the invitation to silence is too poor to give either alms or hospitality. Genuine poverty and simplicity is thus to be her defence against the continual importunities of beggars and the undesirable visits of itinerant nuns who would regale her all night with tales of intrigue. The anchoress is to be content with a household of two for company and for service, an old woman, "not talkative or quarrelsome, neither a busybody nor a tale-bearer" who keeps the door against all comers, and "a strong girl to carry heavy things, to bring in water and wood, cook the beans and vegetables or prepare something more nourishing if sickness demands it" (par 4). The common practice of holding a school for boys and girls at the cell window is not to be tolerated, as being another obstacle to that complete separation from the world which the permanent enclosure signifies. Later in the rule we shall see how those little human tendernesses of smiles and tears and kisses, which the anchoress has thus rigorously denied herself, will find their outlet in her daily converse with her divine spouse, after whose embraces she sighs.

The climax of these opening admonitions with their glimpses of feminine weakness is a paragraph on silence, in which the graver tempo of the Latin and its accumulated sibilants suggest the atmosphere in which the anchoress is to live. It is to be an expectant silence, attendant upon God. "Let her lips be silent that she may speak in the spirit, and let her believe that she is not by herself when alone. For then she is with Christ, who does not choose to be with her in a crowd. Let her, then, sit and hold her peace, listening to Christ and speaking with him" (par 5). This rare, contemplative silence must be experienced to be known—being, as it is, quite different from a mere absence of noise. Not an air of constraint, but an atmosphere of peaceful awareness should, in Aelred's view, be the normal fruit of the recluse's principal austerity. The anchoress, therefore, speaks rarely and then at specified times and under specified conditions, in a voice "neither dour nor fawning". Her parlour rules form a somewhat lengthy appendix to this section. They are very Cistercian in their restrictions on speech, but their purpose, in Aelred's words, is the retention of that tranquillity of spirit and peace of heart which fits the soul to be the dwelling-place of him who "makes his abode in peace". "Not merely silly but even frequent talking destroys this holy state of mind. So you must remember that you are to pursue nothing so much as silence" (par 7).

There is a familiar story of how Anthony the Great was taught by an angel to avoid the psychological dangers of unbroken silence by establishing a rhythm of alternating work and prayer. It is upon a similar principle of discretion that Aelred introduces the question of the anchoress's daily time-table. He quotes St Benedict's dictum that idleness is the enemy of the soul. "But since our mind, which in this life is subject to vanity, never remains in the same state, we should escape idleness by a variety of activities and maintain our peace by certain changes of occupation" (par 9). Apart from the Divine Office, recited on St Benedict's plan, Aelred counsels fidelity to St Benedict's simple and modest principle about mental prayer, that it should be brief and pure.[40] Nightly throughout the year the anchoress reads the *Lives of the Desert Fathers*, or Cassian, to stir her to compunction before she says Compline with the last of the light. A recluse who cannot read is instructed to give herself to longer periods of manual work, broken by intervals when she kneels down for a brief moment of prayer. Apparently she repeats the Our Father many times a day, varying it with any psalms she happens to know by heart. In Lent, which receives a long paragraph to itself, the emphasis on prayer is to be greater. "Let her fall to prayer more readily than usual, more often prostrate herself at the feet of Jesus, excite herself to compunction by the frequent repetition of his most sweet name" (par 11). The image behind this little phrase is almost certainly that of the penitent Jerome as he pictures himself in the desert "prostrate at the feet of Jesus",[41] but the recommendation to the tender devotion of the prayer of the name of Jesus belongs to a newer world. In the same way, the comparison of Lent to the period of our mortal life occurs in more than one place in Augustine[42] and reappears in Rabanus Maurus[43] and other writers before the twelfth century, but in Aelred it is transformed by a new and vivid awareness of the symbolic power of the liturgy that makes it seem quite fresh. The whole passage gives an impression of continuity with a past that has remained vital and fertile.

Summary norms for diet and clothing bring to a close this first part of the *Life of Recluses*, which has been in the main concerned with the recluse's outward mode of life adapted "not to the fervour of antiquity, but to the tepidity of these times of ours". The transition to the second part occurs at what is virtually a new beginning, strongly reminiscent of the prologue to St Benedict's rule. "But let her now hear my words and understand them, whoever she be that, renouncing the world, shall choose the solitary life and, wishing to be hidden, shall seek not to be seen and like a dead woman to be buried in a cave with Christ" (par 14). The sepulchre image is classical in this connection, deriving as it ultimately does from St Paul's concept of the Christian life as a burial through baptism and a rising again to a new kind of life.[44] The recluse's purpose is to please God in body and soul in the perfect Christian life. Her virginity is to be preserved in view of a true espousal with Christ. "He has already chosen you as his spouse, but he will not crown you unless you are proved. As the scripture says: 'He who is not tried is not proved.' Virginity is the gold, the cell the furnace, the blower the devil, and temptation the fire. The flesh of the virgin is the earthen vessel in which lies the gold to be purified." The whole of this long passage, which includes a description of Aelred's own early struggles to attain the virtue of chastity, is redolent of the ascetic tradition of the old north of England, where Cuthbert had sung his psalms in the cold waters of the sea and Aelred, like his friend Godric, castigated his body with prickles.[45] "My God, what crosses, what tortures that poor wretch suffered, until at last the love of chastity was granted to him. Now a sick man, he is growing old, yet even so he does not flatter himself that he is safe" (par 18). Like the dove that sees the approach of the hawk in the mirror of the waters, Aelred's sister is to defend herself against the attacks of the devil by frequenting the living waters of the scriptures. Thus Aelred calls an image from the bestiary to his aid,[46] and he thinks of a memorable phrase of Jerome as he goes on to tell her to let sleep overcome her thinking of the scriptures.[47] She is to let something from scripture be her first thought on waking, just as she lets a word of scripture, lodged in her memory, give savour to her sleep. This long discourse on the preservation of chastity is rounded off with the story, evidently of one of Aelred's own monks, who both in health and sickness avoided that false discretion about bodily penance which "more easily tolerates the flame of desire than a rumbling stomach." Not that Aelred would speak in dispraise of discretion, which Cassian, whose phrase he quotes, had called mother and nurse of all the virtues, but he would emphasize the importance of that true discretion which prefers the soul to the body.

Having said so much, Aelred is aware of the danger of pharisaism which so relentless a quest of virginal perfection always involves. In developing his thoughts on the fundamental safeguard of the virtue of humility, he inveighs against the occasion for private vanity which is possible even in the possession of a beautifully furnished cell, its walls adorned with pictures and carvings, its oratory gay with embroidered hangings. Taking his text from the bridal psalm 44, he insists that the recluse's glory must be "all from within", her soul being adorned with the varied hues of the virtues, her spiritual gown trimmed with the golden fringe of charity. A completely fresh, non-scriptural image then occurs to him, which is so perfectly adequate to his thought that he digresses for a paragraph.

The altar in the oratory of the anchorage must be adorned with its white linen cloths, symbols of purity and simplicity. Let the recluse only consider with what labour the linen used for this purpose is prepared. It is steeped, dried, beaten, combed twice over before spinning, and even then it has still to be boiled over the fire before it reaches its final beauty. So it is with our souls. We are buried first with Christ in the waters of baptism, which takes away our sin but not our weakness. We must therefore dry out our evil dispositions by abstinence and, like the flax, be beaten with the buffets of many temptations. The teeth of discipline gradually comb out all our superfluities, though our lightest faults must still be eradicated by daily confession. Patiently we must endure with prolonged perseverance, just as the spinner draws out the linen thread. "And further, just as fire and water are applied to it that it may acquire a greater beauty, so we must pass through the fire of tribulation and the waters of compunction before we reach the refinement of chastity" (par 26). This elaborate interpretation of the symbolic significance of the altar linen is to be the recluse's substitute for all decorations. "Upon your altar let a picture of the Saviour hanging on the cross suffice, that it may remind you in whose sufferings you share, that its open arms may invite you to his embraces which shall be your joy, that his naked breast may give you the milk of delight to comfort you." From this consoling reminder of the "maternal breasts"[48] of the sacred humanity, the eye may pass to pictures of the Virgin Mother and the virgin disciple on either side of the Rood, where they stand united through the Son in an unbreakable bond of charity.

As Aelred has already said, it is this charity, binding all the virtues in one, which should give the finish to the wedding-dress of the spouse of Christ. It will be the theme of the closing pages of his letter. But, since charity is two-fold, love of God and innocence and beneficence towards our neighbour, he will not avoid considering first of all the charge that Martha brings against Mary. "The one offered service, the other fostered love". Unlike those who dwell in monasteries, "whose life has not a little in common with that of Martha", the recluse, whose condition is that of Mary, seems to be so totally cut off from the world that she may well be asked: "What good, then, do you do for your neighbour?" (par 28). In reply Aelred quotes a phrase of St Gregory, "Nothing is richer than a good will". Following the sequence of Gregory's thought in this sermon for St Andrew's day,[49] Aelred shows how the recluse's rightness of will towards all men makes her compassionately sensitive to their needs, and so moves her to pour out her prayers for them.

Bind, then, the whole world in one embrace of love. There remember and rejoice with all the good. There behold the evil and weep for them. There look on the afflicted and oppressed and have compassion. There let the plight of the poor, the complaints of the orphans, the desolation of widows, the sorrows of the sad, the needs of pilgrims, the vows of virgins, the perils of those at sea, the trials of monks, the worries of superiors, the fatigue of warriors all come to your mind. Open the breast of your love to all these, for these shed your tears, for these pour forth your prayers.

Prayer is Aelred's final concern, and in the advice he has to give we see his pastoral method reach its perfection in a scheme of great simplicity. "So that the sweet love of Jesus may increase in your heart you will need a threefold meditation, of things past, present, and to come, that is to say remembrance of things past, experience of things present, and reflection upon things to come" (par 29). The remembrance of things past is to take the form of a meditation upon the incidents of the Gospels conducted in a manner with which the exposition of the passage on *Jesus as a Boy of Twelve* has already made us familiar. But now we have a whole series of touchingly conceived models, extending from the Annunciation of our Lady to the Resurrection of our Lord, in which the recluse enters into the scenes she is contemplating, following the characters about, sympathizing with their feelings and reactions, and making their situations her own, so that their life becomes hers. Here it is that all the life of the affections which the ascetic rule has damned up, may flow out freely in connection with divine things. Not that the recluse can always expect to experience the joys of God's presence in her prayer. "Sometimes it will seem to you that he averts his eyes, closes his ears, and hides his desirable feet. Nevertheless, do you cry in season, out of season: "Why do you turn away your face from me?" (par 31). The centre even of the life of prayer on earth can scarcely fail to be the cross where "the mediator of God and men, hanging midway between earth and heaven, joins highest to lowest, earthly things to heavenly."

Meditation on the mysterious workings of grace in their own souls in the present moment prompts Aelred to a bitter lament for the sins of his youth, for which his sister often reproached him. "You therefore rejoice in the riches which divine grace preserved for you: upon me lies the burden of making whole again what was broken, finding what was lost, mending what was torn" (par 32). There is no doubt that on themes like this Aelred's mind very easily succumbs to the feeling of pessimism in one aspect of Augustine's thought. His reflections carry him forward to consider the hidden things of predestination and the perils of the Last Judgement, when one and the same face of Christ appears so different to the blessed and to the damned. Yet, all his fears put aside, it is with thoughts of eternal bliss in the vision, knowledge, and love of God that the work closes.

When all the reminiscences are gathered and the echoes caught there is no work in which the true complexity of Aelred's ascetic inheritance can be better appreciated than in the *Life of Recluses*. Until the theme of personal destiny comes up, Augustine is, as we should expect, of less importance here, and Jerome, whose influence is ultimately the most vital, has been absorbed by an imagination formed in the atmosphere of Cassian, Palladius, and Gregory. The rule of St Benedict, above all, reduces to moderation and harmony any tendencies to exaggeration in this tradition. From the Celtic background of his home country comes Aelred's inclination to value the more extreme and violent forms of bodily asceticism, but this is tempered by the warmer, gentler piety which had been on the increase in fervent monastic circles since the eleventh century, and particularly flourished among the first generation of the monks of Cîteaux. If the contradictions are not always quite satisfactorily resolved this may sometimes be due to a feeling of timidity and inexperience in dealing with the problems of women. What is chiefly sure and original in Aelred's treatise is his personal grasp of the psychology of the early stages of affective, discursive prayer and this is the most convincing evidence of his genius as a teacher and pastor of souls. The last part of the work has neither the depth and richness of the meditations that William of St Thierry wrote for his novices, nor the clear organization of Hugh of St Victor's more old-fashioned *How to pray*.[50] But there can be little doubt that the unsophisticated would find Aelred the easiest and plainest guide to the practical question of how to begin to pray. In that field his influence, though often hidden under other names or working its way through anonymously, continued for generations. The other works he produced by responding to the claims of the life of the Church in the north were of more specifically local interest, but in his *Life of Recluses* Aelred unwittingly discovered something that would survive in the life of the Church at large even when the anchorholds he knew fell into disuse.

7

Darkness and Light

Bouts of acute pain from arthritis and the stone had compelled
Aelred reluctantly to submit to mitigations in his daily régime from
about 1157 onwards, and to find a way of being as little trouble as
possible to everyone else on these occasions. His solution had been
to erect an outbuilding near the common infirmary of the abbey,
where he could have a fire and be close enough to benefit from the
provisions normally made for the sick. There, at the same time, he
could conduct the business of the monastery and see members of his
community without disturbing anyone else. In this place, when he
was at home, he more and more worked and talked and prayed.

By Walter Daniel's account there must have been a good deal of
talking to be done. Rievaulx had been growing steadily all through
Aelred's life and, towards the end, on the greater feast days, when
the lay brothers came in from the granges, the church was crowded
with the brethren "like bees in a hive". There were, we are told,
one hundred and forty monks and five hundred lay brethren at the
time of Aelred's death.[1] Inevitably the life of this large community
converged upon the abbot's simple lodging, where there was an
atmosphere of freedom in which to talk about scripture and the
problems of monastic life and anything that was wholesome and
interesting. For Aelred, who had often had to be very firm with
himself in his search for the appropriate self-discipline, knew the
importance of allowing the immature their root-room. He understood, as his own ascetic teaching makes clear, when to insist but,
unlike the disciplinarians whom Walter Daniel calls "silly abbots",
Aelred never crushed the spontaneity of his young men. Twenty or
thirty at a time could be found any day round his bed, or sitting on

it, talking to him. Walter Daniel says that they felt able to be so
open with him that they were rather like children with their
mother.[2] This comparison is not merely sentimental, as we may
judge from another friend and admirer of Aelred who also stresses
his "maternal" quality in a literary conceit which shows that the
connotation of the underlying image is the same for him as it would
have been for Aelred himself. Reginald of Durham in his *Little
Book on the Wonders of St Cuthbert* says in his dedication to
Aelred: "We have often drunk the milk of refreshment and consolation from the breasts of your maternal compassion. For from
the three fingers of your kindly paternal rule hangs the regulating
vessel of discretion".[3] In this vessel the feelings of the heart are
given their proper proportions in the mixture that makes up a
whole and happy life. It was thus that, in his subjects and in all who
came under his spiritual influence, Aelred tried to ensure the conditions for healthy, unstultified growth.

The compassion which was the fruit of Aelred's own physical
and moral trials did not, however, go with softness or idleness. To
the end he was thinking and working, new projects were being
conceived and new ideas coming in. In the one book which Walter
Daniel says Aelred left incomplete, the late fifth-century mystical
writer whom the Middle Ages knew as Dionysius the Areopagite
is mentioned by name[4] and, although the phrase cited from him is
difficult to identify satisfactorily in the Latin translations Aelred is
likely to have known,[5] its presence confirms the impression that
Aelred never ceased to be subject to the theological influences that
affected his contemporaries. It may be doubted if the intermediaries
by which these influences were brought to bear on him will ever be
easy to isolate but that, in spite of Aelred's avowals of lack of
scholastic formation, they are there cannot really be questioned.

It is true that Aelred's purposes were rather different from those
of the masters in the schools, and therefore it is not the evident lack
of an adequate philosophical discipline alone that makes his work
On the Soul seem incomplete. It may even be doubted whether
Walter Daniel was correct in supposing that Aelred had intended
to add anything more to the text as we have it,[6] since it comes to
what seems to be a natural conclusion. But he was certainly not
mistaken in seeing that by Aelred's own standards the work was
unfinished. It raises so many problems that it leaves unresolved, and
cites so many authorities it never sufficiently digests or uses that it

really fails, from an unwonted decline in skill, in its simple and central purpose, which is clearly stated near the beginning of the opening dialogue. The pivot of the Cistercian emphasis on experience was the belief that even looking within, to its living self, in a spirit of faith, the soul could discover in its own nature a mirror of, and so a point of contact with, divine things. It is by this route that in the first part of the *Mirror of Charity* Aelred conducts his reader beyond created things to their source in the intimate inner life of God himself. A similar programme is announced for the work *On the Soul*. But it begins with a problem raised by some remarks of Augustine, "that man of inimitable subtlety", in his work on the literal sense of the book of Genesis. From the beginning to the end of his career Aelred's use of this book becomes apparent at every important point and there is good reason to think that it meant for his general theological formation all that the *Confessions* meant for his imaginative and devotional life. But Aelred had little of Augustine's philosophical penetration and here, in his dialogue *On the Soul*, he seems to get lost in his own puzzles and questions. The purpose of asking them is, however, plain. Remembering the stock answer that boys at school used to be taught about the presence of God in the universe, the burden of the opening of the dialogue *On the Soul* is to insist that the soul is present in the body, not as a material object is in place or even simply as something is present where it acts, but rather with the whole essence of its being. This comparison is possible because the soul is utterly simple and uncomposed. That God is like this, Aelred's interrogator cannot doubt, but what it means to say this, either of God or of the soul, he cannot understand. "And so", Aelred replies, "cleaving to the foundation of faith about the things of God, let us ask about the soul which is made in God's image, how it can be the sort of thing it is; for perhaps if you discover the image you may more easily find him of whom it is the image". It is doubtful if the moment of insight which seems here to be promised is ever reached, so complex and sometimes so hesitant are the paths by which the argument travels.

The first part of the dialogue is really a prolonged discussion of Aelred's definition of the soul and the consequences which flow from it. "The soul of man in its present state is a kind of rational life, changing with time but not with place, immortal in its own way, and capable of bliss or misery." It is said to be a kind of rational life, Aelred explains, to distinguish it from the life which trees or animals have, and it is changeable not as things that move from one place to another, but as things that evolve in time. Thus it is immortal, not as God is immortal, but with a life whose potentialities for good or ill have yet to be realized. Unlike qualities which can be separated from it as, for instance, wisdom, the three powers of memory, understanding, and will are of the very substance of the soul. How this purely spiritual soul, which is envisaged as merely using the body, comes into being, no view is put forward, since Augustine himself never reached a definitive position on the question. More important still, no satisfactory explanation of the soul's relations with the body and the life of sensation can be offered without admitting the existence of some principle joining soul and body which is neither physical nor exactly spiritual, but with "a capacity for spirit". To fail on this point is not, perhaps, so discreditable, for better minds than Aelred's were to struggle with this question for another century while they remained caught in the embarrassments created by Augustine's neo-Platonism.

Aelred is more at home with the imaginative aspects of his topic. During the first dialogue the sense of wonder evoked by the power of memory, on which Augustine expatiates in the tenth book of his *Confessions*,[7] has been suggested by Aelred as one of the most vivid ways of appreciating the differences between the rational soul and those of plants and animals, and it is with this "huge hall of the memory" that Aelred begins his second dialogue. Where in another work on the soul Augustine had invoked the memory of distant Milan as an illustration of the indifference of this spiritual power to the bounds of space,[8] Aelred speaks of the view of the great city of London seen from across the Thames, with St Peter's abbey to the West, the Tower to the East, and the old church of St Paul between. This astonishing storehouse of impressions has "a capacity for God". Through the right use of the human power of understanding upon the matter which memory presents, a man can come to share in God's truth, since everything true is in the mind of God in a pre-eminent way.[9] When, by the help of grace, the will freely embraces the truths which the mind thus delivers, man draws near to the life of God.

These perspectives are clear enough. But then Aelred embarks upon a discussion of the role of grace in relation to free choice, which occupies most of the latter part of the second dialogue. This in itself is an obscure and difficult subject and Aelred suffers from his somewhat confusing inheritance about it. St Bernard had tried his hand at it in his treatise *On Grace and Free Choice*,[10] and many parallels to what Aelred has to say in his dialogue *On the Soul* can be cited. On the other hand, it never becomes entirely clear whether what Aelred says could not be as adequately explained simply in terms of Augustine's many discussions of this topic. Certainly it is from Augustine that the traditional Platonist proofs of the soul's immortality from its rational activity are resumed.[11]

Aelred's closing dialogue is concerned with the separation of the soul from the body and its state after death, again a theme with an immense range of speculative possibilities. The consideration of the moment of separation is made the occasion for a classification of the soul's powers which has been emerging in the course of the previous discussion. This classification into the sensitive, imaginative, and intellectual powers bears some resemblance to Aelred's classification of types of vision in his homilies *On the Burdens of Isaiah*, and may ultimately derive from brooding on the same passage of Augustine on Genesis which there appears to be the source.[12] But then there are further difficulties, and how to explain the pains of the damned, and what may be the kinds of pain they experience, presents many problems. Only the state of the blessed is clear. The good soul finds God in itself at the moment of death, and this brings it immediate happiness and the bliss which is appropriate to its particular mansion in heaven. There are saints, who

> see us in him, in whom we live and move and have our being; there they hear us, there they wait upon our desires, there they behold our needs, nor are there lacking angels to present our prayers to God. Therefore let us honour, praise, and glorify the saints with what devotion we can, contemplate as far as possible their bliss, imitate their lives, and desire their company. For they care for us and pray for us with a devotion proportionate to the fact that they know they cannot be complete without us.

Rare in this treatise are the moments in Aelred's familiar vein and, by comparison with the exquisite little work on the same subject by his able English Cistercian contemporary Isaac of Etoile,[13] the dialogue *On the Soul* must be regarded as no more than a brave attempt at a task which might well have proved beyond Aelred's powers, even had they not been failing as he wrote. His gifts lay in another direction, not in the world of speculations and abstractions, but in the world where men move and act, led on perhaps by an ultimate vision, but passing through conflicts and obscurities and alternations of darkness and light. All Aelred's understanding of this seems to be embodied in what is perhaps the most interesting of the works of these closing years, which rightly enjoyed a European popularity in monastic circles.[14] It still deserves an interpretation as imaginative and yet as disciplined as that which Aelred used to explain the difficult texts of Isaiah which he took as his starting-point.

The *Homilies on the Burdens of Isaiah*[15] grew, as Aelred tells us in his dedicatory epistle, out of an Advent sermon. The prophet of the Incarnation, as he is regarded in liturgical usage, was a natural choice for the season, and his words led Aelred to say in his exposition of the prophet's meaning a great deal about the human situation. When the work was at last finished Aelred sent it with a commendatory letter to Gilbert Foliot. He, having failed to be appointed archbishop of Canterbury when the king nominated Becket in 1162, had been translated from the see of Hereford to London in 1163 in order to be near the king in the tensions with his new archbishop which were already beginning.[16] Aelred's relationship with the austere opponent of Thomas of Canterbury is not quite clear, his letter, in spite of its effusions about love and friendship, being almost as enigmatic on this question as the character of the bishop himself.[17] The letter reads like a plea for the friendly good offices of an important bishop who, although much occupied with the king's business and his own pastoral cares, is still said to find time to study the scriptures. Foliot's unexpected kindness to Aelred on some unspecified occasion in London encourages him to think that Gilbert will be prepared to look through the work and either give it the approval of his learned authority or suggest corrections and emendations. It was evidently to the friendship of the Gilbert who, whatever his political affiliations, had the reputation of remaining a good monk, that Aelred aspired, and it was certainly a very characteristic product of the monastic milieu that Gilbert received, alive with a vitality wanting to his own clear but colourless writing.

To Foliot Aelred explains how the homilies came to be written.

When, some time ago, I had briefly discussed in chapter the prophetic burdens of Isaiah, touching summarily upon each, I yielded to the wish of many of the brethren, whose profit it is my duty to serve, that I should continue at greater length. And so, starting with the burden of Babylon and passing on through the burden of the Philistines to the secrets of the burden of Moab, having committed thirty homilies to writing, I stayed my pen, lest I should run on in vain. Prefixing that sermon which became the occasion for the rest I have written, I have therefore appended nineteen homilies on the burden of Babylon, three on the burden of the Philistines and nine on the burden of Moab, being prepared at your discretion either to stop at this point or to carry on.[18]

Whether there was any reaction from Gilbert Foliot we do not know, but the work which follows the epistle conforms to this description. The introductory Advent sermon runs through the eleven burdens or oracles of Isaiah "touching summarily upon each". As Aelred draws to his conclusion he says, "We have broken as best we could this barley bread but, hurrying on to other things, we have dropped many fragments in the breaking. Do you therefore who have leisure, whom Christ has kept free from these cares, gather up the fragments that remain lest they be lost." When he had finished, the brethren evidently suggested that no one was better fitted to take up this invitation to explore the matter further than he himself. He accordingly returned to his starting-point and began the task in a form so ample that, like the *Mirror of Charity*, these homilies soon found their abbreviator.[19]

It was no mean undertaking for a sick and busy man to perfect so elaborate a work, half treatise and half commentary. Only a few years previously another English monk, Osbern of Gloucester, a Benedictine of some literary attainments, had dedicated to Foliot a work on the book of Judges,[20] but it attempts nothing that could be compared with Aelred's discussion of the question of prophetic vision in the second of his homilies. Where Osbern is largely working up his sources, Aelred is clearly using his as a means of thinking out the problems anew. With the aid of some dictionary of scriptural proper names, he also works hard on the text itself. One of the homilies is so stiff with these interpretations that the abbreviator lost courage before it. It is hard to find a true parallel to work of this kind among Aelred's Cistercian contemporaries. The English Gilbert of Holland commenting the *Song of Songs* has followed St Bernard's method in producing homilies which may be rich in scriptural allusions but which are seldom embarrassed by the limitations of the text he is expounding. Aelred, on the other hand, is working much closer to the methods of an old-fashioned exegete trained in the school of St Gregory. From the point of view of technique we are probably nearest to the right atmosphere in the homilies on Ezechiel preached a few years after Aelred's death by Robert of Cricklade, the elderly prior of St Frideswide's, Oxford.[21] Apart from systematic commentary, schematic treatments of biblical themes, akin to that of this group of oracles, were much in vogue among monastic writers of this generation and a comparison will be sufficient to show that it was no more than a coincidence that a Benedictine in Styria, Gottfried, Abbot of Admont, a contemporary of Aelred, should have written a group of homilies on the ten burdens of Isaiah.[22]

In the fine exordium to the first of his thirty-one homilies, Aelred admirably communicates the enthusiasm and generosity of mind which he could bring to an ambitious task.

> "Woe to me if I preach not the gospel"; especially since I do not doubt that, whatever progress I make in spiritual teaching or the under-standing of the scriptures, is not so much given to me as sent to you through me. I neither ascribe this to my merits, since I am a sinner, nor to my scholastic training since, as you know, I am almost un-schooled, nor even to my study or hard work, since I am rarely at leisure and often engaged in business. So it all comes from God, committed to me, transmitted to you, that "he who glories may glory in the *Lord*".

Aelred clearly knows how one should set about the sort of project he proposes, and he feels that in his experience of spiritual things and in his reading of the scriptures he has received something to give. Yet, however the gift came to him, it looks as though it must have had some interesting human intermediaries, about whom we still know too little. The confidence and deft simplicity with which Aelred handles the difficult philosophical notion of participation in this opening homily poses probably the most intriguing problem in the evolution of his thought. It is not only the extremely felicitous use of a text from the book of Wisdom that suggests the atmosphere of Greek theology. The eye falls at once upon the statement in the first sentence that God is "the primordial and efficient cause" of all things, past, present, and to come. Has Aelred found this word "primordial" in Hugh of St Victor's *De Sacramentis*;[23] or where William of St Thierry made his contact with the Greek theology of Dionysius the Areopagite in the Latin versions and interpretations of the ninth-century John Scotus Erigena?[24] That there is some point of contact with such a world can hardly be doubted. According to Aelred, the being which all things have is a participation, or share, in the being of God, who is the "being of all things that exist". This last phrase is the very one which, in his work *On the Soul*,[25] Aelred cites as coming from Dionysius. The distinctive manner of participation proper to the rational creature was wisdom, by falling away from which man became like a foolish beast. But because he still exists and lives, the possibility of being reformed by him who formed him is still open. This reformation is brought about by the schooling of faith, hope, and charity, a learning which is ministered to us by those whom wisdom has made "friends of God and prophets".[26] Hence it is that holy scripture is the fount of all learning. Shorn of the philosophical complexities with which he surrounded it, this was also Erigena's conception of the role of scripture in the scheme of descent from and return to God.[27] However we are to explain it, it is certain that if there are elements of Augustine in Aelred's exposition of these ideas, they have been transformed by contact with the world of the Pseudo-Denys. Unfortunately, by contrast with William of St Thierry, these influences seem to have come to Aelred too late and to have been too restrained in their effect to enable us to push our investigation too far. Nevertheless, here at the beginning of his *Homilies on the Burdens of Isaiah* they seem to have had a notable effect on his sense of theological perspective.

Life in the monastic milieu, which is essentially one of struggle with evil spirits and with the snares of one's own thoughts, creates a special need to renew one's relish of divine things by the rediscovery of the innumerable thoughts which may be drawn from even the most familiar page of scripture. In this business of redeeming the time and making sport of it, Aelred begins with a statement of the subject of the selected passages seen as a whole. The prophet Isaiah is describing the bringing low of a number of cities and their peoples, and telling how for some among them these trials, in which God separates night from day and light from darkness, are spiritually remedial. The trials or burdens of which the prophet speaks may thus be regarded from two points of view, in so far as, for those who undergo or suffer from them, the same events produce different results in different people, according to the dispositions of divine providence. For some these trials are certainly a burden, but one from which they survive, spiritually chastened and refreshed. Some, on the other hand, go through them all to no purpose. They neither believe in God's good intentions towards them nor conform themselves to the issue he seeks to bring about. Like the people of Israel of old he "lets them follow the desires of their own hearts". In the end the burdens crush them, and God lets them perish along the path they have chosen. Aelred intends to apply this very fundamental spiritual doctrine to each of the prophetic burdens in turn. It seems clear to him that since the discerning between good and evil was effectively accomplished by the coming of Christ, this coming and the discernment which results from it is the real matter of which the prophet is ultimately speaking. The explanation of the allegorical and tropological meaning of the text will enable Aelred during the course of these homilies to show how the underlying spiritual purpose of the oracles works out at two other levels. The moral conflict of the Christian and monastic life, which the tropological meaning reveals, is thus seen in the setting of the historic and apocalyptic conflict of the Church, of which the literal sense is an allegory. It is their absorption with these broad theological and spiritual vistas that gives these homilies their peculiar strength and impressiveness.

Aelred's second homily is a very fully argued discussion of the manner in which the prophet saw the burdens of the peoples. Against the word "vision", the first word in the prophecy of Isaiah, glossed bibles generally give a division which derives from the closing book of Augustine's *De Genesi ad litteram*,[28] as do the remarks of many monastic commentators. But Aelred attempts something more ambitious and more personal. The possibility that some early scholastic treatise has played its part here cannot altogether be excluded, but it is most probably on the basis of the discussion in which Augustine outlines his threefold scheme that Aelred devises his sixfold scheme of types of vision. He discerns the vision of the physical senses, imaginative and fantastic vision, spiritual vision, and rational and intellectual vision. This scheme introduces clear distinctions between the various workings of the imagination in normal and morbid psychology and in deliberate phantasy. For the spiritual vision which takes place in rapture he uses both Augustine's word "ecstasy", and the more characteristic word of the Cistercian school *excessus*. His distinction between the function of reasoning and the intuitive grasp of understanding, while not implicit in

Augustine's discussion here, is in conformity with his views in other places. Aelred discusses most of Augustine's scriptural examples of the way visions occur and adds several more of his own. His conclusion that it is not the vision, of whatever kind it be, that makes the prophet, but the perception of its significance "in the very truth", is substantially Augustine's. But the emphasis on truth as light, which suggests to Aelred a transition to the kindred question of passive states of contemplation, probably owes something to the thought of Gregory.

Nowhere in his writings, when he is speaking of his own experience, does Aelred ever refer to anything that would make him seem spiritually singular, and it is typical of his reserve that on this occasion he illustrates what he wishes to say from the experience of a convent of Gilbertine nuns. Since Watton was the only Gilbertine monastery near Rievaulx, it may well be of these nuns that Aelred is once again speaking. The steps by which the subject is introduced are important. In "the truth itself", which is the source of the prophet's knowledge, all things past, present, and to come are simultaneously present. This is why the Lord tells his disciples that the Spirit he is sending them will lead them into the truth of the many things he wishes to say to them which they cannot bear now. It is expedient for them that he should go away, because it is their attachment to his physical presence and the sound of his voice that prevents their forgetting all these bodily things and ascending to that region where the Spirit speaks to man's spirit in the light of truth. Aelred himself knows of a Gilbertine nun who achieved this degree of detachment and who, kindled with desire for heavenly things, one day experienced in prayer a sweetness which extinguished every other thought. She attained to the ineffable light of that truth in which she "began to know Christ no longer according to the flesh but according to the spirit." Her long and frequent raptures became the subject of comment and, as the result of earnest prayer, were eventually shared by other members of the community, with the notable exception of one nun who, besides doubting the genuineness of the experiences, was not prepared to pay the price of the detachment involved. One Good Friday, however, she too was granted the experience for just long enough to believe that her sisters were telling the truth, though she herself, as a weak one, asked to be allowed to descend to the spiritual vision of Christ hanging on the Cross. This effective experience of seeing the

Saviour looking at one with kindly eyes from the Cross is not to be despised. The prophets too had visions of this type. Aelred's real point in telling the story is to say, with St Bernard and other later mystics, that mystical experiences of this latter kind are not the highest and may easily be deceptive.

On the other hand, the Cross in itself is the sign of separation which in the fullness of time the preachers raise in Babylon, the city of confusion. To preach the Cross is, as St Paul says, the apostolic commission, but it is a mystery. "You have hidden the mystery of your Cross, Lord Jesus, from the wise and prudent and revealed it to little ones. These are the little ones, the humble apostles and apostolic men, who are commanded to lift up a sign on the dark mountain."[29] Whether we interpret Babylon as the world in which the apostles first preached the gospel message, or as the soul which is still subject to the warfare of the vices, the Cross becomes a burden which must either be accepted as a purification, or rejected as an insupportable obstacle. Even those whose ordered rhythm of life leads them from the sermon to reading and from reading to prayer, still have much to suffer as long as the relics of sin survive in them, "as we learn by daily experience." "This is why many of the disciples of Christ hearing the mystery of the Cross 'turned back and walked no more with him' ".[30] The Christian life and the monastic life is certainly a life of difficulty, but the monks are not alone. The angels are with them in choir and present at their prayers and reading, driving off, if they wish it, the evil spirits and opposing their wiles. "Happy soul his who, as he sings, is kindled with the desire of him of whom he sings and, moved to devotion and tears, speaks to those whose presence he feels in the spirit, saying, "Daughters of Jerusalem, tell the Beloved that I languish for love". Such a soul, the friend of God, and the dwelling-place of the Holy Spirit, becomes in its troubles like the "lily among thorns". Here the vivid insistence upon the angelic presences looks back to monastic antiquity, and would have seemed familiar enough to Bede,[31] but the allusions to the *Song of Songs* give the language a new feeling of intimacy and tenderness.

The first five of the *Homilies on the Burdens of Isaiah* form a group which fulfils clearly the procedure Aelred has forecast, and at the same time exemplifies the outlook characteristic of the Cistercian movement in its first vitality. It is evident that it was not only to a properly monastic past that these Cistercians of the first

generation looked back. Their devotion to scripture gave them a
strong feeling for apostolic times and the unadulterated apostolic
message, and their natural sympathy with contemporary Gregorian
reforms led them, like many theoreticians, to idealize the first
freshness of the early Church. They wanted to experience all over
again what they believed it to have been. We get a lively impression
of this in Aelred's ninth homily where he speaks of the difficult
period of persecutions as being also a time "when a certain happy
necessity compelled almost everyone to be perfect." This is contrasted with those signs of the approach of the last days which
appear when the stars of heaven no longer give their light. The two
great stars, the sun of the priesthood and the moon of kingship, no
longer keep their seasons. Kings meddle in priestly matters and
bishops rule over the night of secular affairs. Let them look back to
the example of Gregory, Augustine, Hilary, Martin or, nearer
Aelred's own world, to Cuthbert, Wilfrid, John of Beverley, and
Dunstan. The present is a favourable time to flee from the midst of
Babylon and take to the heavenly tents.

It is in the temporary dwellings of the monastery, where Christ
"makes men of one manner dwell in a house", that there are called
together from near and far those who are to fight in that warfare
which is always going on, as it were, behind the scenes on which
public events are played out. Those who are called "come from far"
if, on account of their addiction to the vices, they come from the
"region of unlikeness"[32] to Christ the perfect image of the Father,
who never loses his likeness. The monks recover their likeness to
him by the practice of the virtues, chastity chiefly by interior solitude, charity by voluntary poverty, possessing nothing either
physically or spiritually precisely as their own. They must work
while it is day, with the thought of the night of death, in which no
man can work, before them, and taking the will of God for their
daily food.

But these are the paths of personal reconciliation with God,
through the redemptive work of the cross taken as the standard of
daily living. Already in his explanation of the gospel On Jesus as a
boy of twelve Aelred had spoken with touching warmth of another
reconciliation which in his mind was intimately bound up with the
thought of the last days.[33] Here again in his fourteenth Homily on
the Burdens of Isaiah his principal theme is the final conversion of
the Jews, that unhappy people whom their Christian oppressors

keep in the subjection of servitude. The gentiles will then lead the Jews into their place, that is the Church, and their respective roles will be, as it were, reversed.

For there will be such joy to the peoples that those whom they now have as persecutors and masters they will then have as servants and handmaids in love, as the Apostle says, "serve one another through love." "And they shall make them captive that had taken them." The prophet's words describe, as it seems to me, that mutual love with which the Jews and gentiles shall take hold of and embrace each other as with arms of love.

Even at the time he wrote these words it cannot have been unimportant that these were the thoughts of the abbot of a large monastery about twenty miles from York, a city where Jewish culture then flourished and where there may even have been a school of literal exegesis.[34]

The world in which these painful separations occur and persist is a world in which the ramifications of evil are a great mystery. Once again Augustine on Genesis provides the starting-point for the discussion of the fall of Lucifer and its consequences. From the passage of Augustine Aelred cites comes the notion that the devil too has a body, the counterfeit of the mystical body of the Church, through which the mystery of iniquity works itself out.[35] None of these ideas are reproduced like dead flowers stuck in a scrap-book, as they are apt to appear in the works of mere compilers. In Aelred there is always a vital apprehension of the great theological themes and they give an urgency to his burning digression on the papal schism which was to last many years after he was dead.

In 1169 Alexander III sent a letter to the Cistercian General Chapter thanking the Order for the support it had given him from the beginning.[36] The news of his election in 1159 had been brought to England by messengers from the Cistercian abbot Philip of Aumone,[37] and it is clear from his digression on the Council of Pavia, which opened on 5 February 1160, that Aelred was accurately informed about the facts. At first only the two cardinals John and Guido had supported the anti-pope, Cardinal Octavian, who took the name of Victor IV, although five names eventually appeared on the document emanating from him, as against "fifteen or more" on that of Alexander. Cistercian Chapter in 1160 and 1161 had taken its decision in favour of Alexander, so that Aelred's personal expression of his adherence was backed by its authority. The argument he uses to calm any doubts or hesitations in the minds of his monks is that "Christ is ever in the faith of Peter", whose universal rule was proclaimed even on human authority by the Donation of Constantine. The Church is built up, not with walls and stones, but on the apostolic succession. Hence the Roman clergy are called "cardinals", being rather like the pillars on which the world is supported. This is customary language enough since the days of pope Leo IX,[38] though the suggestion that the cardinals are the successors of the apostles in the way that the pope is successor of St Peter is somewhat startling. This point is not, however, germane to the contention that the force of apostolic authority rests with those who elected Alexander since they were clearly in the majority, and where he is there is the Roman Church. "Wherever we can plainly discern the Roman Church, there is my heart."

Whether the external trials are of European significance, like the schism, or merely arise from local hardships, like the failure of the harvest, they are only the counterpart of that interior condition of struggle in which the monk habitually lives. Those who endure this struggle virtuously eventually sleep the sleep of victorious kings. They pray that the Lord will arise with a merciful severity against their vices, and ease the yoke of evil habit under which the sons of Adam labour from their mother's womb until the day when they return to the womb of the earth, the mother of us all. "It is a truly great sign of divine mercy, brethren, when he does not spare us in the present." This is even true of the carnal temptations that God permits them to suffer. These could, perhaps, lead the soul to a state of despair, but God intends them for its profit.

I speak to the experienced. At the beginning of our conversion, amidst grave temptations of flesh and spirit, when the spirit of fornication sometimes consumes us, when anger flares up, when appetite tickles the palate, it might seem almost impossible to bear it all, especially when the instability of youth and the cunning diversity of temptation suggests a fall from weakness that would be easy. What, then, shall we reply to spirits that suggest such things? What shall be our hope, what our refuge? The Lord has founded Sion, and in him his poor shall hope. Look, my beloved, should someone be over-taken in any fault, or unusually troubled by some temptation, let him consider whether, before the fall, his heart was not perhaps lifted up. For if he weeps for the cause of that sin, he will more easily obtain pardon for what he has done. Then, indeed, he will become poor of spirit and humble of mind, for it is not those who trust in their own riches, but those who glory in their Christian poverty who shall hope in the Lord.

This emphasis on humility, and on the spiritual poverty which comes when the soul, emptied even of attachment to its own virtues, is prepared to receive the riches of God, goes with the doctrine that the trials to which the soul is submitted plunge the soul into a night of purgation. The purpose of this is to cleanse the very springs of its activities at a level where the wounds of original sin make it prone to actual sin. "Then the kind Saviour acts like the best of physicians and first cuts off the cause of these ills. Delights are gradually withdrawn, and when hard and sad things follow, sensual pleasures also disappear. Thus a man, forced to return into himself, finds there nothing clear, nothing fair, nothing to please or soothe him, but everything dark, everything obscure, everything full of dread and night and gloom." Many souls are not brave enough to bear with all this and they try to run away from it. If they do not see that all their ascetic efforts have been leading them in this direction it is often because they do not cleave to the sovereign remedy in every difficulty. "If within, where God sees, the heart of man is converted to God and contrite, soon the heart of God is converted to him." From the deep well of the scriptures God calls out to us in our hearts and unlocks his secrets.

So, brethren, to the extent that outward persecution or inward confusion makes us sad, the divine consolation of holy scripture makes us happy. "For what things soever were written, were written for our learning; that through patience and the comfort of the scriptures we might have hope." I tell you, brethren, nothing contrary can happen, nothing sad or bitter occur, which does not either quickly go, or prove more easy to bear as soon as the sacred page explains it to us. This is the field into which the holy Isaac went forth to meditate, the day being now well spent, where Rebecca coming to meet him softened with her gentleness the affliction that was his. How often, my good Jesu, the day draws towards evening; how often to the daylight of some little consolation the dark night of some insupportable sadness succeeds. All is turned to weariness; everything I see a burden. If someone speaks, I scarcely hear; if someone knocks, I am hardly aware of it. My heart is hardened like a stone, I cannot speak, my eyes are dry. What then? I go forth to meditate in the field; I turn over the Holy Book, and write my thoughts on the tablets, when suddenly thy grace, good Jesu, like Rebecca running up, disperses the darkness with its light, drives away weariness, breaks my hardness. Soon to sighs tears succeed, and heavenly joy comes with tears. Unfortunate are those who, when some sadness troubles them, do not go out into this field that they may be happy.[39]

This was the final maturity to which Aelred came. With his fellow Cistercians he had taken delight in the joys of spiritual things, in the happiness of loving and feeling loved by God and man. But the ultimate things did not seem to him to be so tangible. It was not in his own judgement or experience that he placed his confidence, but in the common things of the Christian faith as they are to be found in the life of the Church and the teaching of scripture.

Segor, that is the Church, is aptly said to be a three-year-old calf, that is, in its third year, the first year being before the law, the second under the law, the third under grace. One could alternatively understand the first year to be under the patriarchs, the second under the prophets, the third under the apostles. Now this kind of animal is rich in milk and, where its offspring are concerned, extremely affectionate. For, unless it is deceived by some trick, it does not allow another's calf its teats, nor will it normally give its milk unless its own is there. These things are suitably adapted to our mother the Church which, rich in the milk of charity and agreeable doctrine, takes those whom she has not regenerated with water to be strangers and unworthy of the holy mysteries. It can also be said to be three years old, for strengthened in faith, hope, and charity, it "grows to maturity, to the measure of the stature of the fullness of Christ".[40]

The theological virtues of faith, hope, and charity have thus become the centre of Aelred's life, and his reading of scripture leads him to see the hand of God in all that happens, in all the factors that shape his life both without and within. It is this which vindicates his courage in using everything and rejecting nothing about his life, his temperament, his weaknesses even, all his half-forgotten past, though he may not always have seen at the time how it could be of use in the service of God. What the result amounts to he does not attempt to judge, and when he meets the brethren of his monastery for the last time he takes only the common Christian criterion of what it is to love God.

I have lived with a good conscience among you for, as you see me lying here at the point of death, I call God to witness that, since I took this religious habit, I have never, for any man's malice, detraction, or argumentativeness, been consumed with a feeling against him which could have lasted the day in the house of my heart. Always loving peace and the good of the brethren and my own soul's tranquillity, by the grace of Christ I have commanded this soul of mine that the sun should not go down while anything continued to trouble my heart's patience.[41]

We need not doubt that he spoke the truth when he said "God, who knows all things, knows that I love you all as I love myself and truly, as a mother after her sons, 'I long for you all in the bowels of Jesus Christ'". No one could ask for a more Christian ending.

8

Epilogue

✤

Every movement of protest inevitably develops its own style and language. The more negative these are, the more empty its conventions look in retrospect and the harder it is to recapture what it was that made them credible. If the movement generated by the group of monks at Cîteaux had been a mere reaction against the devitalizing tendencies of a religious institution, buildings with the impressive sureness of Fontenay, Le Thoronet, and Poblet could never have come into existence. They express a conviction of purpose which only a group of like-minded men can realize. In their simplicity they make articulate a search for authenticity which is presupposed to the literary remains of its ablest interpreters. Richard of Fountains may never have written a book, but when he says that he and his fellow rebels at St Mary's, York are concerned not just to get back to the primitive observance of Benedictine rule, but rather to "the ancient gospel of Christ which precedes all rules",[1] he puts his finger upon the nerve of the movement. Other generations and other times will see this desire as having rather different implications, but not even the Franciscan movement, which awoke, and still awakes, a similar nostalgia ever succeeded in reinterpreting the apostolic message with such theological power and completeness as the outstanding early Cistercian teachers did.

Unique historical factors brought this about, and among them the coincidence in time of a number of remarkable men whose varied gifts it would have been harder to recover without their own surviving writings. These, nevertheless, bear witness to only one aspect of their lives. The immediate impact of their personalities is necessarily something at which we can only guess. Their lives were larger than their books. William of St Thierry, describing his first impression of Bernard at Clairvaux, says: "When I entered that splendid cell, and reflected upon the dwelling and the one who dwelt there, God knows the place struck me with the kind of reverence I would have had on going up to the altar. I was touched by such a tender regard for that man, and so strong a wish to share with him in that poverty and simplicity, that if the choice had been given to me that day I should have desired nothing so much as to remain with him there always, to serve him.[2] These may sound like the extravagant praises of an uncritical admirer, but they must be seen in the context of the thought of a man who belonged in spirit to the movement before, contrary to Bernard's counsel, he himself became a Cistercian at Signy in 1135. While still a Benedictine abbot, William had expressed in memorable phrases in one of his meditations for novices the notion of a liberty that breaks through any self-imposed programme or convention and permits the spirit to translate his intentions into a language whose meaning does not require words for its expression. "These are thy simple servants with whom thy talk is wont to be. In going to thee, they do not put their trust in the chariots of their own ideas or the horses of their own strength, but only in the name of the Lord. And therefore thy wisdom, arranging everything perceptively for them, they arrive by a little way and with a light burden at their destination, where horses and chariots are no more. They do not form or conform themselves to thy love by subtle methods, but thy love, finding in them the simple material, forms and conforms them to itself in desire and in fact. Thus, apart from what lies hidden—wealth and riches in the house of a good conscience—not by any artificial effort, but as it were by a natural fittingness, the interior light is reflected upon their faces, so that their countenance and bearing in its attractive simplicity acts as a stimulus to love and often, at a mere glance, urges rough and uncultivated souls to the love of God. Thus, when nature returns to its origins, without a teacher are they taught of God."[3]

This is spiritual doctrine in a classical tradition, yet with an uncommonly vivid sense of distinctively Christian values in their bearing upon human life as a whole. William, whose explicit awareness of the traditions of East and West alike was something quite exceptional even among his learned contemporaries, is capable of writing with a degree of intuitive concentration which must set him apart among theologians of eminence. Yet it is ultimately in defence of a thoroughly humane equilibrium that his notable intellectual gifts are exercised. Bernard has a cooler power, yet the finest of his writing pursues similar purposes with an astonishing compression and lucidity. The notion of "nature returning to its origins", of the experiential discovery of one's true situation in relation to things human and divine, is the ascetic programme of Bernard's little treatise *On Loving God*. It has perhaps been too little noticed that, grounded as it is in St John's conviction of knowing oneself as loved before requiring of oneself to be loving, informed with a synthesis of the patristic doctrine of man, and explicitly integrating into its structure every article of the creed right through to the resurrection of the body, this brief and tightly-constructed treatise is the last classic of undoubtedly major stature in the West to display in a single coherent vision the spiritual doctrine of the undivided Church.

It is an essential feature of a school of writing whose devotional "tone" is thus not yet separated from an integral view of Christian theology that it carries within it coherent principles of pastoral practice. If one emerges from an extended reading of early Cistercian sources with an impression of having encountered very individual personalities nurtured in a common climate of thought, this at once suggests a wider world of less articulate people within their ambiance, valued and appreciated for themselves. The characteristic which Aelred appears to have shared with Bernard at his best, with William of St Thierry and with the delightful Guerric of Igny, is a fatherly concern for his brethren, discreet enough to be genuinely brotherly. In the presence of these early Cistercian abbots one is haunted by a background of so many unknown eyes and faces. There is no way of recovering what all this meant, but it is certainly of more human importance than anything of which books can tell.

The facts and figures, the tangible monuments which remain, of this creative generation are too secure and too imposing to be explained as the expression of a transitory illusion. The Cistercian style was new but its inspiration was, as they rightly believed, an old one which, from time to time, puts out new leaves. The monastic tradition is only really comprehensible when it is expounded by men for whom it is a living, contemporary experience. It communicates itself by affinity. This communication, whereby one spark ignites another, was evidently what the finest abbots of Aelred's generation made possible. No one can legislate for it, and it is as the authentic transmitter of an ultimately unwritten tradition that St Benedict in the second chapter of his *Rule* tells us "what kind of a man the abbot ought to be". At the end of his *Rule* he logically pointed behind him to the desert Fathers of whom stray, exemplary stories and sayings were preserved, as they in their turn, "with more truth than the nineteenth century suspected",⁴ pointed back to the apostolic Church as the source of their way of life. In these terms it is possible to watch Aelred slowly discovering what kind of a man *he* ought to be.

Aelred's *Pastoral Prayer* comes nearest to being the embodiment of what his personal ideal finally came to be. It defies adequate analysis. As far as the Prayer's more or less explicit ancestry is concerned, it is impossible to improve upon the judgement of Dom Wilmart that its closest kinship is with the prayers of the eleventh-century Benedictine John of Fécamp.⁵ Yet this does not argue a belief in any definite literary relationship. The paternity is of another kind. There is one aspect of Aelred's thought that belongs to the universal monastic tradition as it was mediated by fervent monks nearer his own day than the saints and Fathers to whom he consciously looked back, just as whole areas of his mind reveal an uncritical acceptance of the cultural conventions of the secular milieu with which he was most familiar. If Aelred's *Pastoral Prayer* could almost have been written by John of Fécamp, but not quite, this is because a new degree of self-consciousness and self-evaluation has broken through, as in his explicit acceptance of the possibility that even his defects and weaknesses might have their positive part to play in his own sanctification and in his prayerful service of others. It is impossible not to link this unreserved oblation of spirit before God with that notion of his soul as the "handmaid of the Lord", to which Walter Daniel's *Life* and one of his own sermons allude. Unlike William of St Thierry and Bernard, whose theological interests are wider, Aelred is first and foremost the abbot at the service of his brethren, and it is perhaps natural to find his closest affinity of spirit with the charming Guerric, Abbot of Igny, of whom only a small collection of sermons were spared from the flames by sons too devoted to destroy them as their author had wished. In Guerric the "handmaid" theme also appears in a manner of which Aelred would certainly have approved. "I am the handmaid of Christ", says the abbot in one of his Christmas sermons, "be it done unto me according to thy word. Yet I shall show myself to be, as far as possible, a mother in love and concern, though always remembering what I am. O, my brethren, this name of mother is not the prerogative of superiors, though upon them particularly falls the duty of maternal care and devotion. It is common to all of you who do the will of the Lord. For all of you are indeed mothers of the Son who is given to you and in you, whereby you have conceived in the fear of the Lord, and brought forth the spirit of salvation. Take care, then, holy mother, take care of the newborn child, until Christ be formed in you."[6]

Of the great Cistercians of this early period none saw the claim of Christ upon him as being so extensive over the entire range of his human ties and possibilities as Aelred did. The list of his writings reads like a list of debts to God and men paid off over the years according to the circumstances and in the manner that each would have wished. The childhood years are woven into the work on the Hexham saints. Youthful idealism informs the *Battle of the Standard* and the *Genealogy of the Kings*, where the fact and fiction of the Anglo-Norman world make a mirror of Christian chivalry to hold up to a future king. Nearer his more mature concerns are the long letter to his anchoress sister, and closer still the meditation composed for the young Ivo of Wardon and the dialogue *On Friendship* itself. Yet even here, where the note of intimacy is struck, the effective stimulus reveals itself as the personal claim of others. In the lives of Ninian and Edward the Confessor the courtesy of the response extends even to the style, where the rhythmic prose that the taste of the times required in such a context is apparently effortlessly produced from some store of literary observation. The programme had been laid down in principle in the *Mirror of Charity*, but its working out was a more elaborate and exacting affair than even that most complex of his works. To him might be applied the unexpected words of another more gifted writer[7] of much later times, who consciously struggled to make something of similarly individual endowments. "A Man's life of any worth is a continual allegory—and very few eyes can see the Mystery of his life—a life like the scriptures, figurative."

BIBLIOGRAPHICAL NOTE

The numbered notes provide a guide to the complex bibliography concerning Aelred, but the following list suggests some of the more readily available editions and English versions of Aelred's works for the convenience of the general reader.

LATIN TEXTS

The edition *Aelredi Rievallensis Opera Omnia*, published in three volumes in the *Continuatio Medievalis* of the *Corpus Christianorum* by the monks of Steenbrugge will, when complete, become the standard edition and give an integral text of the *Genealogia Regum* for the first time.

Critical texts (with French translation) are also available in the series *Sources Chrétiennes*, no. 60 (*De Jesu Puero*) and no. 76 (*De Institutione Inclusarum* and *Oratio Pastoralis*).

The *Patrologia Latina* of J. P. Migne gives in vol. 195 texts of the *Speculum Caritatis, De Amicitia, Vita Edwardi, De Sanctimoniali de Wattun*, together with most of the Troyes collection of Aelred's sermons, while vol. 184 gives the *De Jesu Puero*.

ENGLISH VERSIONS

G. Webb & A. Walker offer the following: *On Jesus at Twelve Years Old* (London 1956); *Letter to his Sister* (London 1957) (This version begins only at par. 14 of the critical Latin text); *The Mirror of Charity* (London 1962).

There are several versions of the Pastoral Prayer: tr. by a Religious of C.S.M.V., with Latin text (London 1955); tr. in *The Way*, July 1964, pp. 231-5; tr. Sister Rose of Lima, introd. A. Hoste (Steenbrugge 1967).

H. Talbot, *Christian Friendship* (London 1942) is perhaps still the most engaging of any of the English versions of a complete work of Aelred. There is another version by M. F. Jerome (New Jersey 1948).

Very few of Aelred's sermons exist in translation as a whole, but a good example is the Assumption sermon tr. A. Storey in *The Tablet*, Aug. 1951, pp. 91-2, under the title "The Castle of the Soul".

Passages from Book I of the *Mirror of Charity* are attractively presented and translated in E. Colledge, *The Medieval Mystics of England* (London 1962) pp. 105-21.

NOTES

LIST OF ABBREVIATIONS

Acta SS	The Bollandist *Acta Sanctorum*
Amic.	*De Spiritali Amicitia*
Anim.	*De Anima*
Bibl. Aelr.	*Bibliotheca Aelrediana* ed. A. Hoste (Steenbrugge 1962) with supplement to 1967 in *Cîteaux*, 1967, pp. 402–7.
CS	Camden Society
CCCM	*Aelredi Rievallensis Opera Omnia, Corpus Christianorum, Continuatio Mediaevalis* (Three volumes announced)
EHR	*English Historical Review*
Flor. Wig.	*Florence of Worcester* ed. B. Thorpe, vol. II
Inst.	*De Institutione Inclusarum*
Past.	*Oratio Pastoralis*
PL	*Patrologia Latina, Cursus Completus* ed. J.-P. Migne
Pink.	Pinkerton's *Lives of the Scottish Saints* ed. W. M. Metcalfe (Paisley 1889). Two volumes
Priory	*The Priory of Hexham* ed. J. Raine, SS, 1963, vol. 1
Puer.	*De Jesu Puero*
Reginald	Reginald of Durham's *Libellus de Admirandis Beati Cuthberti Virtutibus*, SS, vol. 1, 1835
RS	Rolls Series
Sanct.	*De Sanctis Ecclesiae Hagustaldensis*
Serm. Ined.	*Sermones inediti B. Aelredi Abbatis Rievallensis* ed. C. H. Talbot (*Series scriptorum S. Ordinis Cisterciensis*, I, Rome 1952)
Spec.	*Speculum Caritatis*
Stand.	*De Standardo*
SS	Surtees Society
Symeon	*Symeon of Durham* ed. T. Arnold, RS, 2 vols., 1882–5
VA	*Walteri Danielis Vita Ailredi Abbatis Rievall'* ed. F. M. Powicke (London 1959); to appear in *CCCM*, III

NOTES

Chapter 1

1. VA, p. 62
2. VA, pp. 18–19
3. *Commentarii Scriptoribus Britannicis* (Oxford 1709) I, p. 200
4. VA, p. 60
5. The Latin presents difficulties and the MSS offer variants, but the general sense is clear. *Serm. Ined.*, p. 81
6. *Past.*, 7. CCCM 1
7. VA, p. xxxiv
8. *Sanct.*, cap. 2 (*Priory*, pp. 177–81)
9. See G. Baldwin Brown, *The Arts in Early England* (2nd edn, 1925) pp. 149–84
10. *Gesta Pontificum*, RS, p. 255
11. *Sanct.*, prol. (*Priory*, p. 175)
12. *Symeon*, I, pp. 56–7
13. *Symeon*, I, p. 65
14. Reginald, pp. 22–8
15. *Symeon*, I, p. 78
16. The account which follows is based on *Symeon*, I, 87 ff and Reginald, 57 ff
17. *Priory*, appendix, p. viii
18. *Symeon*, I, pp. 98–101 and *Symeon*, II, pp. 188–90
19. Reginald, pp. 30–2
20. *Symeon*, II, p. 190
21. *Symeon*, I, p. 106
22. *Symeon*, I, p. 108–10
23. *Symeon*, I, pp. 116–23
24. *Sanct.*, cap. xi (*Priory*, p. 191)
25. Reginald, pp. 28–9
26. Reginald, p. 84 ff
27. See *Victoria County History*, Durham, vol 3, pp. 93 ff
28. VA, p. 72
29. *Inst.*, 32
30. *Sanct.*, cap. xi (*Priory*, pp. 192–3)
31. *Symeon*, II, p. 34
32. *Post scholars praepropere relictas* (*Acta SS*, August, I, p. 258, par. 32)
33. *Amic.*, prol.

34. See G. W. S. Barrow, "From Queen Margaret to David I: Benedictines and Tironians", *Innes Review*, 1960, pp. 22–38, and note Lawrie's *Early Scottish Charters*, no. 144 (p. 157), the *form* of which may be spurious, though its substance is confirmed by *Liber de Calchou*, nos. 413 and 409

35. VA, p. 3
36. *Acta SS*, August, I, p. 252, par. 15
37. Malmesbury, *Gesta Regum*, RS, II, p. 477
38. *Acta SS*, par. 47, *Eloquens Gallicae et Anglicae Linguae*
39. For VA, pp. 3–4 see G. W. S. Barrow, *Regista Regum Scottorum*, I, (Edinburgh 1960), pp. 32–3
40. R. L. Graeme Ritchie, *The Normans in Scotland* (Edinburgh, 1954), p. 250
41. Reginald, p. 1
42. *Inst.*, 18
43. *Forte pessimum desperationis remedium adhibuissem*, Spec. i, 28 (PL 195, col. 531–2)
44. VA, p. lxxi
45. Richard of Hexham, *Priory*, pp. 57–8
46. D. Nicholl, *Thurston, Archbishop of York* (York 1964), pp. 127–137
47. See J. C. Dickinson, *The Origins of the Austin Canons* (London 1960)
48. See D. Knowles, "The primitive documents of the Cistercian Order", *Great Historical Enterprises* (London 1963), pp. 199–224
49. *Stand.*, opening tribute to Walter Espec.
50. *Consilio et Concessu Turstini* (Cartulary of Rievaulx, SS, 1889, p. 21)
51. VA, pp. 12–13
52. "Memorials of Fountains Abbey", SS, 1862, vol. 1, pp. 13 ff
53. The other point of view is well expressed in Nicholl, *Thurston*, pp. 157–162
54. VA., p. 10
55. *De Gradibus Humilitatis*, I, par. 2 (J. Leclercq and H. M. Rochais, *S. Bernardi Opera*, vol. III)
56. II, par. 3 and 4
57. *Consuetudines* ed. Guignard, 172
58. III, par. 9
59. IV, par. 13 and 14
60. VI and VIII, par. 19 and 20
61. J. Weatherill, "Rievaulx Abbey; the stone used in its building", *Yorkshire Archaeological Journal*, vol. 38 (1952–5), pp. 333–54.

Chapter 2

1. Epist. 250
2. *Acta SS*, August I, p. 257
3. John of Hexham, *Priory*, p. 139
4. Epist. 346

5. Bernard, Epist. 347, and see C. H. Talbot, "New Documents in the case of St William of York", *Cambridge Historical Journal*, vol. X, 1950, pp. 1–15
6. See D. Knowles, "The case of St William of York", reprinted in *The Historian and Character* (Cambridge 1963) pp. 76–97
7. VA, p. 25
8. The MSS are unanimous on the authorship of this letter and Dom A. Wilmart sorted out the learned confusions surrounding it in 'L'instigateur du *Speculum Caritatis* d'Aelred, abbé de Rievaulx", *Revue d'ascétique et de mystique* xiv, 1933, pp. 369–94, and p. 429
9. Sermon 26 on Isaiah (PL 195, col. 476)
10. Eadmer, *Vita Anselmi*, I, xix
11. *Amic.*, opening discussion of book 2
12. See J. Leclercq, "S. Bernard et ses secrétaires", *Revue Bénédictine*, 61, 1951, pp. 208–29, and A. Squire, "Hugh of St Victor: Selected Spiritual Writings" (London 1962), p. 18
13. See A. Squire, *The literary evidence for the preaching of Aelred of Rievaulx* (*Cîteaux* 1960) pp. 165–79, and C. H. Talbot, "Ailred's Sermons: Some first drafts", *Sacris Erudiri*, 1962, pp. 153–93
14. A. Wilmart, *L'instigateur*, p. 370n.
15. Troyes MS 1838
16. Troyes MS 281, fol. 2v
17. Oxford MS Ashmole 1285, a small, bulky volume, 180 mm. high and 130 mm. wide, with an *ex libris* of the Augustinian Canons of St Mary Overy, Southwark. It consists of a number of pieces of very different origins, dates, and hands, and there is consequently nothing to exclude a Cistercian origin for the text of *Spec.* which occurs between fol. 236–69v
18. Published by A. Wilmart, "Un court traité d'Aelred sur l'étendue et le but de la profession monastique", *Revue d'ascétique et de mystique*, 1947, pp. 259–73. I have given reasons for supposing that the authenticity of this piece must stand or fall with that of the text of *Spec.* in A. Squire, "The composition of the *Spec.*", *Cîteaux* 1963, fasc. 2, pp. 135–46
19. *Acta SS*, August I, p. 258
20. Augustine's "Dilige et quod vis fac" (PL 35, col. 2033) is cited by Aelred as "Habe caritatem et fac quidquid vis" (*Spec.* iii, 35)
21. "Paterna auctoritas, fraterna caritas, propria necessitas"
22. Thus *Spec.* ii and *Spec.* iii, 35 are being considered together
23. Benedict's *paululum* is omitted by Aelred in quoting the Prologue to the *Rule* in *Spec.* iii, 35
24. This version of the passage from *Spec.* ii, 17 is translated from the draft version published by A. Squire in *Cîteaux*, 1963, fasc. 2, pp. 145–6.
25. These words occur only in the final version of *Spec.* ii, 17, and from this point onwards the passages of the full text of *Spec.* (PL 195 col. 501–620, *CCCM*, I) are referred to in brackets in the text.

26. *Adversus Jovinianum*, ii, 5-17, but esp. cap. 11 (PL 23, col. 290-312)
27. These phrases of *Spec.* ii, 24 are undoubtedly a reminiscence of Jerome, Epist. 22, par. 29
28. Now Cambridge University Library MS Mm 4.28
29. Bernard cites Aelred as saying this in the letter commanding *Spec.*
30. W. G. Hoskins, *The making of the English Landscape* (London 1955) p. 81
31. In *Spec.* ii, 17, 18 Aelred seems to have Gregory's Homily 30 on the Gospels (PL 76, col 1220) chiefly in mind, though he probably cites from memory.
32. *Amic.* iii
33. VA, p. 50
34. "Audivi sed heu sero clamantem" (*Spec.* i, 28). Most allusions of this kind have been collected by P. Courcelle in *Les Confessions de S. Augustin dans la tradition littéraire* (Paris 1963) pp. 291-305
35. Tract. 26 in Ioann., par. 2
36. I have been unable to discover any intermediary for the quotation from Juvenal, *Satires* X, 22 in *Spec.* i, 23
37. *De Genesi ad litteram*, xi, 24 is specifically cited by Aelred as his authority in the full text of his Homily 16 on Isaiah. The same work is also the evident source for the idea of the different kinds of kisses in *Amic*, ii. For *Spec.* the *De Gen.* iv, esp. the first twenty chapters are of chief importance.
38. Abelard's *O quanta qualia*

    O what their joy and their glory must be
    Those endless sabbaths the blessed ones see!

    must be one of the most familiar hymns of the period still in use.
39. A list, which it would not be difficult to expand, will be found in E. Rondet, *Études Augustiniennes* (Paris 1933) p. 280
40. A. G. Hebert, *The Throne of David* (London 1941) chap. V
41. Compare *Spec.* i, 20 with *De Gen.*, iv, 2 (PL 34, col. 296-7)
42. William of St Thierry also speaks of a *vis naturalis* in *De Natura et Dignitate Amoris*, cap. 1 (PL 184, col. 379). There are other affinities with the doctrine of William in *Spec.* iii
43. This topic, in relation to the Christian doctrine of love, has recently been much discussed; see R. A. Markus, "The dialectic of Eros in Plato's Symposium", *Downside Review*, July 1955, pp. 219-30; A. H. Armstrong, "Platonic Eros and Christian Agape", *Downside Review*, Spring 1961, pp. 105-21; Thomas Gould, *Platonic Love* (London 1963); A. H. Armstrong, "Platonic Love", *Downside Review*, July 1964; John M. Rist, *Eros and Psyche in Plato, Plotinus, and Origen* (Toronto 1964)
44. See esp. Augustine's discussion of the vocabulary of love in *De Civ. Dei*, xiv, 7
45. *Confessiones*, xiii, 9. The example about trees is Aelred's own.

46. Comparing *Spec*. i, 21–3 with Augustine, Augustine has *Beata creatura* in ref. to the angels. Aelred's *mirabilis creatura* is man.
47. *Conf.* xiii, 15
48. The carnal passions are said to be like furies in *Spec*. i, 26, and like beasts in *Spec*. i, 33.
49. Published by A. Squire, "Aelred of Rievaulx and Hugh of St Victor", *Recherches de théologie ancienne et médiévale*, xxviii, Jan.-Jun. 1961, pp. 161–4
50. *Contra Academicos*, iii, 14 (PL 32, col. 950–1)
51. *Spec*. i, 8. Compare Augustine: "Pedes enim nostri... affectus nostri sunt". Enn. in Ps XCIV (PL 37, col. 1217, 2)
52. *De Doctrina Christiana*, i, 4
53. *De Doct.*, i, 22ff.
54. Augustine cites *Philemon* v. 20 in *De Doct.*, i, 33. Aelred's nearest explicit ref. to this is: "Licet verbum hoc frui destrictius soleat accipi" (*Spec.*, iii, 9)
55. Cicero, *De amicitia*, vi, 22
56. Ambrose, *De officiis ministrorum*, iii, 22 (PL 16, col. 181)
57. This version of *Spec*. iii, 39 is a translation of the text given in British Museum Royal MS 5 B ix, fol. 20rb
58. "Solus cum sola secreto et absque arbitrio non sedeas" (Jerome, Epist. 52, 5)
59. The history of the phrase is traced in the masterly article of E. Peterson, "Herkunft und Bedeutung der μόνος πρὸς μόνον Formel bei Plotin, *Philologus*, N.F. Bd. XLII (Leipzig 1933) pp. 30–41
60. *Symposium*, 217B

Chapter 3

1. *Spec.*, Bernard's letter of command
2. D. Knowles, *The Monastic Order in England* (Cambridge 1963) pp. 247–8
3. *Spec.*, ii, 17. The passage has been translated in chap. 2, see n. 24
4. VA., p. xlv and pp. 27 ff
5. A sermon for All Saints' Day, PL 195, col. 342. All subsequent refs. to sermons by column refer to PL 195
6. VA, pp. 24–5; 30–2; 35–6
7. VA, p. 29
8. *Ecclesiastica anima*, col. 359
9. Col. 220
10. St Paul (1 Cor. 15. 41) quoted in this sense in *Serm. Ined.*, p. 117
11. All Aelred's sermons for St Benedict's feast contain some allusion to this comparison.
12. *Corporalia* and *Spiritualia*. For a collection of Aelredian texts on this theme see C. Dumont, "L'équilibre humain de la vie Cistercienne", *Collectanea S. Ordinis Cisterciensium*, 1956, pp. 177–89
13. Col. 242

14. Col. 306
15. *Rule*, chaps, 2, 36, 53, and see H. Van Zeller, *The Benedictine Idea* (London 1959) pp. 28 ff.
16. Col. 317
17. Col. 295
18. *Serm. Ined.*, p. 126
19. *Serm. Ined.*, p. 171-2
20. Col. 248
21. *Consideratio proprie necessitatis, experientia proprie infirmitatis, Serm. Ined.*, p. 141
22. Col. 325
23. Col. 300
24. *Chronicle of Melrose*, facsimile edn (London 1936), p. 34. Aelred's name as abbot is inserted between the years 1146-7
25. VA, pp. 33-5
26. *Serm. Ined.*, pp. 32 ff
27. VA, pp. 37-9
28. "Thy eyes beheld my unformed substance", Ps. 139 v 16
29. See the tables of derivation in D. Knowles, *Monastic Order*, p. 724. The houses in question here are Wardon (1135), Melrose (1136), Dundrennan (1143), Revesby (1143), Rufford (1146).
30. Reginald, cap. 83
31. *Sermo Habitus ad Clerum in Sinodo Trecensi* (first published by A. Squire, "Two unpublished sermons of Aelred of Rievaulx", *Cîteaux* 1960, pp. 110-16)
32. *Feodarium Prioratus Dunelmensis*, SS, LVIII (1872), pp. lx-lxi
33. VA, p. 35
34. Dugdale's *Monasticon*, vol. V, pp. 352-3
35. VA, pp. 45-6. There is some obscurity as to whether the founder of Dundrennan was Fergus of Galloway or David I; see note on the abbey in D. Easson, *Medieval Religious Houses of Scotland* (London 1957)
36. VA, p. lxxv
37. Reginald, cap. 84
38. Reginald of Durham, *Vita S. Godrici Eremitae*, SS (1845) p. 169
39. See Sir Maurice Powicke's chronology for Aelred in VA, pp. xc-xciv, to which must be added the visit to king David in Lent, 1153 (?) referred to in Aelred's lament for him
40. Col. 233
41. Col. 276
42. *Serm. Ined.*, pp. 73-4
43. Isa. 8. 6
44. *Serm. Ined.*, pp. 158-9
45. Critical text (with French tr.) ed. A. Hoste, *Quand Jesus eut douze ans* (Paris 1958) *CCCM*, I. All refs. to this work which follow in the text are to this edn by section and paragraph
46. VA, p. 41 places it before the *Genealogy of the Kings*, and hence before 1154. Powicke dates it 1153-7 (VA, p. xcvii)

47. See E. Gilson, *La théologie mystique de S. Bernard* (Paris 1934), chap. 2, *Regio Dissimilitudinis* (Eng. trans., London 1940)
48. Documented study of Gregory's teaching on this theme by R. Gillet in *Sources Chrétiennes* edn of *Moralia*, vol 1 (Paris 1952), pp. 72–9, and for the whole subject in antiquity I. Hausherr, *Penthos* (Rome 1944)
49. "Rara hora et parva mora" (*Puer.* iii, 23) quotes Bernard *In Cant.*, xxiii, 15 (PL 183, col. 892)
50. Iugiter dulcis illius nominis recordatio" (*Serm. Ined.*, p. 83)
51. It stands first in a line leading to Ludolph the Carthusian, Ignatius Loyola, François de Sales
52. A. Wilmart, *Le jubilus dit de S Bernard* (Rome 1944) pp. 226–7
53. VA, p. 42
54. MS Trinity College Oxford no. 19. For a discussion of this evidence see A. Squire, "The literary evidence for the preaching of Aelred of Rievaulx", *Cîteaux*, 1960, pp. 165–79
55. MS Troyes 910
56. *Serm. Ined.*, p. 172–3
57. *Serm. Ined.*, pp. 106 ff

Chapter 4

1. CCC, Cambridge, MS 66, p. 33ra
2. Both MSS have the Sawley *ex libris*. CCCC MS 66, pp. 1–114 was originally part of C.U.L. MS Ff. I. 27. pp. 1–40 and 73–252 and will henceforth be referred to as one book. CCCC MS 139 was originally two books, the first ending at fol. 165. Important study of this MS by P. Hunter Blair, "Some observations on the *Historia Regum* attributed to Simeon of Durham", in N. K. Chadwick, *Celt and Saxon* (Cambridge 1963), pp. 63–118 arguing, among other things, that this was a Sawley book, a view subsequently confirmed by the discovery of the Sawley *ex libris* under ultra-violet ray.
3. For the Clairvaux library see the study of Dom A. Wilmart reprinted in *Collectanea Ordinis Cisterciensium*, April, 1949, pp. 101–127
4. N. R. Ker, *English manuscripts in the century after the Norman Conquest* (Oxford 1960), p. 9
5. CCCC MS 139, fol. 1r–16v, an *Historia omnimoda*, ending with Pope Calixtus II, d. 1124 and fol. 46r–48v, a chronicle from Adam to the emperor Henry V, d. 1125
6. p. 112 of essay of P. Hunter Blair cited in note 2
7. *De quodam miraculo mirabili*, CCCC MS 139, fol. 149ra– fol 151vb. Ed. by Twysden in *Historiae Anglicanae Scriptores Decem*, reprinted in PL 195, col. 789 ff. *CCCM II*
8. CCCC MS 139, fol. 135va–140ra
9. B.M MS Cotton Vitellius C viii, fol. 6va–fol. 21vb, discussed and analysed in F. Liebermann, *Ungedruckte Anglo-Normanische Geschichtsquellen*, (Strasburg 1879)

10. *Priory*, p. 64
11. *Priory*, pp. 72–3
12. *Bibl. Aelr.*, p. 169, no. 178, Ailredus de standardo
13. York Minster MS xvi.1.8. (Rievaulx *ex libris* on fol. iiii, finishing incomplete at fol. 199vb *accipe inquit ut....*) Text as printed in R. Howlett, *Chronicles of Stephen* etc. (RS, 1886) vol. 3, pp. 181–99. CCCC MS 139, fol. 136va–140ra, printed in Twysden and reprinted in PL 195, col. 701–12. *CCCM II*
14. CCCC MS 139, fol. 136ra has in red and green a large capital R, the first letter of the Rievaulx text, but it abandons this and proceeds with a text beginning *Anno*.
15. Aelred begins: "Regigitur Stephano circa australes partes occupato" (Howlett's edn, p. 181) and Henry of Huntingdon's *Historia Anglorum*, viii, 7, *continues* with the words "Occupato igitur rege circa partes australes Angliae" (RS edn, p. 361)
16. *Vita Thurstini* in J. Raine, *Historians of the Church of York* (RS, 1879–94), vol. II, pp. 259–69
17. *Priory*, p. 78
18. *Stand.* (RS edn) p. 185
19. Gaimar describes the composition of the history in lines 6436–6457 of *Lestorie des Engles* (RS edn, vol II)
20. *Facundiam quae ei facilis erat, Stand.* p. 183
21. The *Rievaulx Cartulary* (SS edn, pp. 264–5) makes Walter spend the last two years of his life as a monk, dying in March 1155
22. *Flor. Wig.*, p. 111. The sources are succinctly written up in A. L. Poole, *From Domesday Book to Magna Carta* (Oxford 1954), pp. 271 ff
23. Aelred's phrase occurs in *Stand.* p. 196 and Abbo's in *Passio sancti Edmundi*, X (*Memorials of St Edmund's Abbey* ed. T. Arnold, RS, vol. 1, p. 15). That Aelred certainly knew Abbo's work is clear from Reginald, p. 23
24. *Priory*, pp. 90–1
25. Compare *Stand.* pp. 185–6 with Huntingdon p. 183
26. *Stand.* pp. 185–6
27. De Gant appears as a witness to letters of both king David and Thurstan on the occasion of the consecration of Robert, Bp. of St Andrews, in York in 1128 (A. Lawrie, *Early Scottish Charters*, Glasgow 1905, nos. 75 and 76)
28. Robert held the land of Exton in Rutland in David's earldom of Northampton. He witnesses sixteen of David's charters and, next to Hugh de Morville, is one of the most frequent names.
29. David granted these estates to the elder Robert *c.* 1124 (Lawrie, no. 50)
30. *Flor. Wig.*, p. 112
31. Huntingdon, p. 264, is the only other writer who knows of this.
32. There can be no doubt from the context that the word *probitas* means "prowess" here. Compare Caesar's speech in Huntingdon, p. 17

33. Powicke suggests 1155-7 (VA, p. xcvii)
34. VA, p. 41
35. *Spec.*, i, 34
36. The text of this lament was ruthlessly abbreviated by Twysden in his edn reprinted in PL 195, col. 711-38. There is a very careful edn from MS Cotton Vesp. D. xi, a Dore abbey book, in Pink., vol. II, pp. 269-85. New edn in *CCCM* II
37. Pink., II, p. 270
38. "Denique his sacris diebus Quadragesimae cum pro quadam necessitate domus nostrae eius adissem praesentiam, inveni fateor in Rege monachum; claustrum in curia; in palatio monasterii disciplinam" (Pink. II, 278)
39. Pink., 273
40. Pink., 279
41. For all these identifications see G. Barrow, "Scottish Rulers and the Religious Orders, 1070-1153" in *Transactions of the Royal Historical Society*, fifth series, 3, pp. 77-100
42. I owe this point to Dr Otto Pächt. There would seem to have been a Rievaulx tradition about this cross for in the MS from there, now Cotton Vitellius F. iii, there are some verses about it at the foot of the charred pages of fol. 50v and 51r
43. Huntingdon, p. 196
44. *Priory*, p. 169
45. *Gesta Regum* (RS, vol. II), pp. 476-7
46. *Hist. Eccl.* viii, 22 (Prevost, vol. iii, p. 403)
47. Ritchie, *Normans*, p. 302
48. VA, p. 42
49. See esp. R. H. C. Davies, *King Stephen* (London 1967)
50. *Priory*, p. 159
51. VA, p. 41
52. See J. M. Wallace Hadrill, "The *via regia* of the Carolingian Age", *Trends in medieval political thought* ed. B. Smalley (Oxford 1965)
53. For the entire theme see J. Seznec, *The survival of the pagan gods* (New York, 1953)
54. CCCC MS 66, p. 69
55. PL 195, col. 719. Refs. to the *Genealogia Regum* by column are to PL 195. *CCCM* II
56. Col. 728
57. A. Squire, "Two unpublished sermons of Aelred of Rievaulx" (*Cîteaux* 1960) p. 112, lines 71-5
58. Huntingdon, p. 185
59. Col. 731
60. Rufinus, *Hist. Eccl.*, I, ii (PL 21, col. 468-9) or *Decretales Pseudo-Isidorianae* ed. P. Hinchius (Leipzig, 1864) p. 256
61. Symeon, I, pp. 230-34

62. Both edns of the parables ed. R. Morris in *An old English Miscellany* (Early English Text Society, 1872), p. 102. The laws of Alfred ed. F. Liebermann in *Die Gesetze der Angelsachsen* (Halle 1903) vol. 1, p. 16

63. *Memorials of St Dunstan* ed. W. Stubbs (RS, 1874), pp. 104-5

64. Col. 724. This story is unknown even to Alfred of Beverley. A verbatim quotation from Aelred in the earliest *Miracula S. Joannis* (which may be dedicated to him) shows that he is the source of this story. (*Historians of the Church of York*, RS, vol. 1, pp. 263-4). Similar stories of Aethelstan's visits to St Cuthbert in *Symeon*, I, pp. 75-6.

65. Col. 730. Aelred is cited as the authority for this fact in the *Dictionary of National Biography* under *Edmund*.

66. See K. Conant, *Carolingian and Romanesque Architecture* (London 1959), pp. 385-400

67. *The Life of King Edward the Confessor* ed. F. Barlow (London 1962)

68. R. W. Southern, "The first life of Edward the Confessor", E.H.R., 1943, pp. 385-400

69. *King Edward*, p. 81

70. J. A. Robinson, *Gilbert Crispin, Abbot of Westminster* (Cambridge 1911), pp. 24-5

71. See B. W. Scholz, "The canonization of Edward the Confessor", *Speculum*, Jan., 1961, pp. 38-60

72. The letters in MS Vat. Lat. 6024, col. 150v-151v were edited in a rather unsatisfactory manner in F. Liverani, *Spicilegium Liberianum* (Florence 1863)

73. PL 200, col. 106

74. e.g. E. W. Kemp, *Canonization and authority in the Western Church* (Oxford 1948), pp. 82-3

75. Letter in S. C. Robertson, *Materials for the History of Thomas Becket* (RS, vol. 5, 1881), p. 16. But Robertson's dating is untenable. The letter must belong to the winter of 1160-1

76. Epist. 59

77. PL 195, col. 458 ff

78. Epist. 23, 24, 27, 28, 29 in *The Letters of Arnulf of Lisieux* ed. F. Barlow, CS. vol. LXI, 1939

79. Bale's *Index Britanniae Scriptorum* ed. R. L. Poole and M. Bateson (Oxford 1902) p. 13 reads: "Ailredus abbas Rievallis scripsit contra literas episcoporum in concilio Papie congregatorum Lib. 1." This scarcely describes Aelred's excursus in the *Homilies on Isaiah*

80. *Chronicon Anglie Petriburgense* ed. J. A. Giles (London 1845) p. 96

81. Epist. 23

82. PL 200, col. 88

83. Letter in Liverani, pp. 733ff

84. Richard of Cirencester, *Speculum Historiale*, RS, vol II, pp. 319ff

85. *Chr. Ang. Petrib.*, p. 98

86. An ambiguous passage in *Gesta abbatum Monast. S. Albani* RS, vol I, p. 159 has led R. M. Wilson, *The Lost Literature of Medieval England* (London 1952, p. 104) to suppose that Laurence wrote a life. But this is unlikely
87. VA, p. 41. (The Latin has an entirely technical sense)
88. *Bibl. Aelr.*, p. 102
89. *CCCM* II; PL 195, col. 740
90. Col. 746. Story cited by Gerald of Wales in *De Principis Instructione* i. RS, vol. 8, p. 129. T. F. Tout also used it, derived through an intermediary, in *Chapters in Administrative History* (Manchester 1920) vol. 1, pp. 72–3
91. Col. 769 ff
92. The texts are all conveniently set out by F. Barlow in edn referred to in note 67, appendix A and B
93. Col. 762 and 777. Aelred's *Life* is thus out of harmony with the theory of M. Bloch, *Les Rois Thaumaturges* (Strasbourg 1924)

Chapter 5

1. *Spec.*, iii, 2
2. *Spec.*, i, 34
3. *Conf.*, ii, 2: "What delight had I, but to love and be loved".
4. *Amic*, prol. (PL 195, col 659) *CCCM* I
5. VA, p. 41
6. Col. 675. Victor IV, the first of the anti-popes elected in the schism, which began in 1159, had died in April 1164
7. VA, p. 39
8. *Tullius de Amicitia* (*Cat. Vet. libr. Eccl. Cath Dunelm* ed. J. Raine, SS, 1838, p. 8)
9. British Museum MS Royal 15 A xx
10. The analysis of the use of Cicero in the edn of J. Dubois, *Aelred de Rievaulx, L'amitié spirituelle* (Bruges 1950) makes this pattern quite clear
11. Notably in *Contra Julianum*, iv, 19
12. Quoting with slight variation Cicero *De amicitia*, par 20
13. Cicero, par 26
14. Proverbs, 17, 17
15. Epist. III, 6 (PL 22, col. 335)
16. Cicero, par. 15
17. See E. Gilson, *Theologie Mystique*, chap. 1
18. Cicero, par. 81
19. Notion based on passages of Augustine like e.g. *De libero arbitrio* ii, 19
20. Aelred quotes *Sermo* 47, 9, 13 (PL 38, col. 303)
21. VA, p. 41
22. *De Genesi ad litt.*, xii, 7 ff
23. Cicero, par. 47
24. *Spec.*, iii, 11

25. A long section is built round the three verses of *Ecclesiasticus*, 22, 25-7
26. *De Officiis*, iii, 22 (PL 16, col. 182)
27. Cicero, par. 76
28. As note 26, col. 183
29. *Conf.*, iv, 8-9

Chapter 6

1. Reginald, pp. 176-7
2. *Bibl. Aelr.*, pp. 153-4, no. 43
3. Now British Museum MS Cotton Vitellius F. iii
4. Rubric from British Museum Addit. MS 38, 816, fol. II
5. *Priory*, p. 194. The date is 1155, new style. A text of *Sanct.* given in *Priory*, pp. 173-203. *CCCM* II
6. *Priory*, pp. 178-80. All subsequent refs. to *Priory* by page are to *Sanct.* unless otherwise stated
7. p. 176
8. See Richard of Hexham, *Priory*, p. 19, and compare pp. 178 and 183
9. pp. 195-8
10. pp. 202-3
11. p. 192
12. p. 184
13. *Priory*, p. 36
14. p. 184
15. p. 200
16. pp. 182-3
17. See W. Pantin, "The pre-Conquest Saints of Canterbury", *For Hilaire Belloc* (London 1942), pp. 146ff
18. *Gesta Pontificum*, RS, p. 328
19. pp. 189-90, B.M. Addit. MS 38,816 fol. 9va supplies Acca
20. *Bibl. Aelr.*, p. 153, no. 43. Text in Pink., vol. 1, pp. 9 ff. *CCCM* II
21. Aelred's mastery of the *cursus* is certainly one of the many things about his formation which needs explaining. The treatise of Peter of Blois on the subject was not written until 1181-5, after Aelred's death. For the context see J. de Ghellinck, *Littérature au Moyen Age*, 2 vols (Paris 1939) vol. 2, pp. 148 ff
22. Pink., vol. 1, p. 11, quoting Bede, *Hist. Eccl.*, iii, 4
23. K. Strecker, "Zu Quellen für das Leben des hl. Ninian", *Neues Archiv.*, xliii, 1920-2, 1-26. The question re-examined by W. Levison, "An eighth century poem on St Ninian", *Antiquity*, XIV, 1940, pp. 280 ff
24. *Cartulary of Rievaulx*, SS, pp. 181-3
25. D. Knowles, *The Monastic Order in England*, pp. 205-7
26. CCCC MS 139, fol. 149. Edn of Twysden reprinted in PL 195, col. 789 ff, *CCCM* II
27. VA, p. 48
28. Critical text of *Inst.* ed. C. H. Talbot (*Analecta Sacri Ordinis Cisterciensis*, 1951, pp. 167-217. This is the text referred to by paragraph. Same editor *CCCM* I

29. *Vita prima S. Bernardi*, 35 (PL 185, col. 248)
30. *Durham Liber Vitae*, SS, vol. 13
31. Reginald of Durham, *Vita S. Godrici*, SS, p. 140
32. *The Life of Christina of Markyate* ed. C. H. Talbot (Oxford 1959), pp. 110–12 and compare p. 15
33. For its influence on the author of the *Ancrene Riwle* see esp. *Ancrene Wisse* ed. G. Shepherd (London 1959) with bibliography.
34. VA, p. 41
35. Jerome, *Epist.* 22 (PL 22, col. 395 ff)
36. PL 103, col. 575 ff
37. The break, which corresponds to Aelred's habitual division between *corporalia* and *spiritualia*, comes at *Inst.* 14, and is the only division in the work which we can be sure was Aelred's own. Not all MSS enumerate paragraphs in the same way.
38. *Opusc.* 15, 3 (PL 145, col. 338)
39. *Inclusa*, normally, *anachoreta* once at *Inst.* par. 3
40. *Rule*, chap. 20
41. *Epist.* 22, par. 7. The influence of this vivid passage is still more evident at *Inst.* par 18.
42. PL 38, col. 1041
43. *De cler. inst.* xi, 20 (PL 107, col. 335)
44. *Vivifica clausus sepultura, Jesu Christi consepeliaris* (Peter the Venerable, Epist. 20, PL 189, col. 100)
45. Bede, *Vita Cuthberti*, X and Reginald, *Vita S. Godrici*, 27 and 37. For the whole topic L. Gougaud, *Devotional and ascetic practices of the Middle Ages* (revised English edn, London 1927) p. 170
46. The dove at the waters must be added to the examples of the use of the bestiary in Aelred collected by J. Morson, "The English Cistercians and the bestiary", *Bulletin of the John Rylands Library*, vol. 39, no. 1, Sept, 1956. Under *Columba* in C.U.L. MS II 4. 26 we read at fol. 41r: "Iuxta fluenta sedet, ut viso accipitre se demergat et sic evadat. Similiter iuxta sanctas scripturas predicatores habitant ut viso impetu et temptatione diaboli in illis scripturis demergatur".
47. Epist. 22, 17
48. Compare *Inst.* par. 31 and *Spec.*, ii, 19
49. PL 76, col. 1094
50. William of St Thierry, *Meditativae Orationes* ed. M.-M. Davy (Paris 1934) for the first twelve, a thirteenth discovered by J.-M. Dechanet, *Guillaume de Saint-Thierry* (Bruges 1942) pp. 193–9. Hugh of St Victor, *De modo orandi* (PL 176, col. 979)

Chapter 7

1. VA, p. 38
2. VA, p. 40
3. Reginald, pp. 1–2
4. *Anim.*, ii

5. Only two ninth-century translations could have been available to Aelred, Hilduin (*c*. 832) and Erigena (*c*. 867), but the phrase may be derived at second hand; see *Dionysiaca* (Paris 1937)

6. VA, p. 42. *Anima* edited from the only four MSS, all English, by C. H. Talbot, *Aelred of Rievaulx: De Anima, Medieval and Renaissance Studies*, supplement I (London 1952). Same editor *CCCM* I

7. *Conf.* x, 8

8. *De quantitate animae*, 5 (PL 32, col. 1040)

9. Doubtless depending on *De Civ. Dei*, xi, 10–11 (PL 41, col. 326–7)

10. *De gratia et libero arbitrio* (Leclercq-Rochais edn, vol. III)

11. Sources seem to be *De immortalitate animae*, 3–4 (PL 32, col. 1022–1024, and *De Civ. Dei*, xiii, 16 (PL 41, col. 388)

12. *De Gen ad litt.* cited by name in *Anim.*, iii

13. *De anima* (PL 194, col. 1875 ff), see G. Webb, "An introduction to the Cistercian *De Anima*", Aquinas Paper, no. 36 (London 1961)

14. MSS are numerous and widespread even today, and there were once many more; see *Bibl. Aelr.*, pp. 57–60

15. Among the old editions the only satisfactory one is that of Aelred's first editor the English Jesuit, Richard Gibbon, *Apud Viduam Laurentii Kellam, sub signo Agni Paschalis* (Douai 1616). This was reprinted at Douai in 1631 and Paris in 1654. It was included in the *Magna Bibliotheca Veterum Patrum*, tom. xiii, Cologne 1618 and the *Maxima Bibliotheca Veterum Patrum*, tom. xxiii, Lyons 1677. For the convenience of those to whom only the abbreviated version of Tissier in PL 195 is available, I give, where possible, a col. ref. *CCCM* I

16. Since the work is dedicated to Gilbert Foliot as bishop of London, it must have been completed after April 1163

17. "Friendship, like letter-writing, was fashionable among twelfth-century churchmen. The result is that it is extremely difficult for us to discriminate between the language of acquaintance and the language of intimacy." A. Morey and C. N. L. Brooke, *Gilbert Foliot and his letters* (Cambridge 1965) p. 13

18. Aelred evidently speaks of "thirty" homilies as a round figure, though his own enumeration makes it clear that there are thirty-one. Tissier's edn, by counting the introductory sermon as the first in the series, alters the enumeration.

19. It does not seem necessary to repeat here the argument I have adduced for regarding Tissier's text as an abbreviation in A. Squire, "The literary evidence for the preaching of Aelred of Rievaulx", II, *Cîteaux* 1960, pp. 245–51

20. British Museum Royal MS 6D ix fol. 73ff. The work must have been completed after 1148, when Foliot became bishop of Hereford.

21. Pembroke College, Cambridge, MS 30 and Hereford Cathedral MS O. iii. 10. The sequence of liturgical feasts mentioned and several refs to the recent martyrdom of St Thomas of Canterbury suggest a date one summer soon after 1170.

22. PL 174, col. 1157 ff. The ten burdens are compared to the ten senses of body and soul, one homily for each. Aelred's scheme is entirely different. Gottfried became abbot of Admont in 1138; d. July 1165

23. *De sacramentis*, i, par. 2a, cap. 1–3 (PL 176, col. 205–7)

24. For a study of this question see work of Déchanet in note 350, appendix II

25. *Anim*, i and first homily on Isaiah (PL 195, col. 363)

26. *Wisdom*, 7, 27

27. e.g. compare *De divisione naturae* i, 3 and iv. 2 (PL 22 col. 443 and 744)

28. lib. xii (PL 34, col. 453 ff)

29. PL 195, col. 372

30. Col. 381

31. See Alcuin, Epist. 284 ed. E. Dummler *Monumenta Germaniae Historica*, Epist. vol. iv, p. 443

32. Col. 391, see p. 68

33. *Puer*, ii, 12

34. For the Jews in York at this period see R. Loewe, "The medieval Christian Hebraists of England", *Jewish Hist. Soc. of England,* vol. xvii, p. 225

35. *De Gen ad litt*, xi, 34 (PL 34, col. 441)

36. For discussion see J. B. Mahn, *L'ordre cistercien et son gouvernement des origines au milieu du XIII siècle* (Paris 1945), p. 139

37. PL 200, col. 1359

38. See Stephen Kuttner, "Cardinalis: the history of a canonical concept", *Traditio*, vol. iii, 1945, pp. 129 ff

39. Col. 476

40. Col. 467

41. VA, pp. 57–8. The discourse may embody a reminiscence of the *Vitae Patrum*: "From the time I took my habit, I have let none go to sleep who still had something against me, and I have never gone to sleep with an enemy in the world" (trans. O. Chadwick, *Western Asceticism*, London 1958, p. 50)

Chapter 8

1 See p. 18

2. *Vita Prima S. Bernardi*, vii (PL 185, col. 246)

3. *Meditativae Orationes*, xii, ed. M.-M. Davy (Paris 1934) p. 278

4. Chadwick, *Western Asceticism*, p. 13

5. A. Wilmart, *Auteurs Spirituels et Textes Dévots* (Paris 1932) p. 289 n. 2

6. *In Nativitate Domini, sermo IV* (PL 185, col. 38)

7. John Keats; letter cited by R. Gittings, *John Keats* (London 1968) p. 5

INDEX

Abbo of Fleury, 78

abbot, responsibilities of, 53–4, 57, 60–6

Abelard, 39

Acca, St, library of, 115

action: alternation with contemplation, 55–6; identified with monastic observances, 59, 120, 123

Aelred (Ailred): birth, 4; family and education, 3–14, 53, 98–9, 112–13; adoption by king David of Scotland, 12–14; lifelong devotion to St Cuthbert, 5–7, 64–5, 112, 141; becomes monk at Rievaulx, 19–22; made novice-master, 24–5; abbot of Revesby, 53; abbot of Rievaulx, 61; journeys, 24, 64–6; unique historical interests, 74; essentially Norman outlook, 13–14; political affiliations, 87; doctrine of two swords, 89; number of sermons, 61, 70; interpretation of Benedictine Rule, 27–30; view of responsibilities as abbot, 53–4, 60–66; *corporalia* and *spiritualia*, 55–6, 120; angels and devils, 137, 140; ascetic symbolism of Annunciation, 2–3, 150–1; experience of oneself, 60, 143; classical ascetic norms, 35–7; importance of Incarnation, 46–7; "a churchman's soul," 54, 145; insistence on compassion, 58–60, 63–4; Cross in Christian life, 33–5, 125–7, 139–141; humility, 59–61; image of God in man, 44–5; monastic ideals, 54–64; monastic abuses, 57–8; teaching about prayer, 47, 67–70, 126–8; spiritual sabbath, 39–43; stages of spiritual life, 35–7, 104–111; Holy Spirit, 47, 71, 139; significance of St John the Evangelist, 37, 40, 96, 106, 149; general nature of theological sources, 32; use of Augustine exemplified, 42–50; stylistic influence of Jerome, 30–1; patristic sources, *see* Ambrose, Augustine, Cassian, Gregory the Great, Jerome, Origen; problem of influence of Bernard, 69, 133; classical sources, *see* Cicero, Juvenal, Plato, Virgil; scholastic influences, 43–4, 101, 105, 130, 136, 138; relation to twelfth century, 32, 43, 50, 150; evaluation of individual personalities, 48–9, 55, 59, 64; lament for Simon, 45–6; lament for David of Scotland, 82–6; friend of St Godric, 65, 119, 124; friend of Reginald of Durham, 64–5, 130; maternal quality as abbot, 130, 150–1; final integration of personality, 3–4; characteristics as writer and abbot, 53–4, 58, 60–2, 150–1; sickness, 64–6, 118, 129–30; death and veneration as saint, 1–2, 145–146; individual writings referred to and analysed, *Spec.* (Mirror of Charity), 15, 25–50, 82, 99, 101–2, 108–9, 131, 135, 151; *Genealogy of Kings*, 88–92, 151; *Puer.* (Jesus as a boy of twelve), 67–70, 141, 151; *Stand.* (Battle of Standard), 17n, 74–82; *Nun of Watton*, 74, 117–18; *Sanct.* (On Hexham Saints), 112–15; *Life of St Edward*, 92–7; liturgical homily for St Edward's day, 95; synodal sermon at Troyes, 64–6, 89; *Life of St Ninian*, 115–17; *Inst.* (*Life of Recluses*), 11n, 15n, 25, 69, 118–28; *Amic.* (On spiritual friendship), 12, 26n, 67, 98–111, 151; *Anim.* (On the soul), 130–3;